Co Down

Edited by Chris Hallam

First published in Great Britain in 2003 by
YOUNG WRITERS
Remus House,
Coltsfoot Drive,
Peterborough, PE2 9JX
Telephone (01733) 890066

HB ISBN 1 84460 086 6
SB ISBN 1 84460 087 4

FOREWORD

Young Writers was established in 1991 as a foundation for promoting the reading and writing of poetry amongst children and young adults. Today it continues this quest and proceeds to nurture and guide the writing talents of today's youth.

From this year's competition Young Writers is proud to present a showcase of the best poetic talent from across the UK. Each hand-picked poem has been carefully chosen from over 66,000 'Hullabaloo!' entries to be published in this, our eleventh primary school series.

This year in particular we have been wholeheartedly impressed with the quality of entries received. The thought, effort, imagination and hard work put into each poem impressed us all and once again the task of editing was a difficult but enjoyable experience.

We hope you are as pleased as we are with the final selection and that you and your family will continue to be entertained with *Hullabaloo! Co Down* for many years to come.

CONTENTS

Christ The King Primary School

Searcha Roissetter	19
Shannen McCusker	20
Jamie Hanna	20
Jason Savage	21
Michelle O'Hare	21
Jamie Dougherty	21
Louise Lavery	22
Kim & Sue Dinsdale	22
Lauren Boyd	23
Shane Melville	23
Lauren Morgan	24
Ashleigh Madine	24
Cathy McCormick	25
Gary Murdock	25
Darren Morgan	25
Ashley McConville	26
Nathan Madine	26
Maria Melville	27
John Cowan	27
Declan Byrne	28
Patrick McAlister	28
Nicola Rice	29
Gary McCormick	29
Michael Ritchie	30
Amie Savage	30
Conor Melville	31
John Wilson	31
Stacie Sloan	32
Shannon O'Hare	32
Catriona McEvoy	33
Paul Gilchrist	33
Fiona Morgan	34
Chelsea Russell	34
Stephen Robinson	34

Glenlola Collegiate School

Caroline McEvoy	53
Lydia Collins	54
Sarah Blair	54
Mai Worthington	55
Bryony Gray	56
Sophie Goddard	57
Ciara Edwards	57
Ciara Lucas	58
Ellen Warwick	58
Antonia Clements	59
Kerry Adrain	59
Hannah Sharpley	60

Grange Park Primary School

Adam Murnin	60
Sara Ebbinghaus	61
Katrina Wolsey	62
Patrick Boomer	62
Adam Caughey	63
Paris Aumonier	63
Piers Aicken	64
Rachel Waugh	65
Victoria Finlay	66
Peter Brown	66
Rebekah Tipping	67
Luke Coulter	68
Peter Allen	68
Hannah Campbell	69
Simon Hull	69
Zoë Brown	70
Rebecca McDowell	70
Lydia McMullen	71
Amy Ferguson	71
Oliver Brown	72
Rachel Jones	72
Emily Allen	73
Kathryn Boyd	73

Lianne Mitchel	74
Catherine Kennedy	74
Katie Gillespie	75
Peter Sames	76
Alistair Stoops	76
Owen Glenn	76
Ashleigh McClurg	77
Lorna Bryson	77
Cara Heaslip	78
Victoria Wilson	78
John Agar	79
Simon Brown	79
Suzanne Hinds	80
James Henderson	80

Iveagh Primary School

Emma-Jayne Johnston	81
Gary Elliott	81
Joanna Simpson	82
Robert Bell	82
Karl Liddiard	83
Ross McKee	83
Matthew Loughlin	84
Hannah McKnight	84
Heather Bell	85
Sara Dougan	85
Stephen Sloane	86
Joanna Simpson	86
April Niblock	86
Amy Shannon	87
Ryan Weir	87
Laura Phillips	87
Hugo Harbinson	88
Stewart Gracey	88
Maeve Henry	89
Callum Elias	89

Jonesborough Primary School
                Maille Beth Connolly   90

Millisle Primary School
                Laura Johnston   91
                Hannah McNamara   92
                Ashleigh McCullough   92
                Alex Sword   93
                Dale Adams   94
                Laura McGimpsey   94
                Stephen Rea   95
                Caroline Atkinson   95
                Laura McAuley   96
                Walter Newell   96
                Alyson Mulholland   97

Milltown Primary School
                Andrew Woods   97
                Sarah Hazlett   98
                Sarah McAdam   98
                Aimee Crothers   99
                Matthew Dickson   99
                Amanda Aulds   100
                Adam Johnston   100
                Jenny Wallace   101

Poyntzpass Primary School
                Louise Robinson   102
                Matthew Patterson   102
                Rebekah Denny   103
                Samantha Boyd   103
                Holly Lockhart   104
                Amy Liggett   105
                Victoria White   106
                Neil Thompson   106
                Stephanie Henry   107
                Claire Hamill   107
                Josh Ferries   108

Windsor Hill School

The Poems

A Day On The Beach!

The sky is clear
The air is hot
The water is cold
The sand is not

The beach is full
All having fun
Nothing better than
Being in the sun

There is ice cream for sale
Cold drinks too
You'd better hurry up
There is a long queue

The sun is setting
It's getting cold
It's time to pack
I'll see you soon!

Lisa Green (11)
All Children's Integrated Primary School

Tea

I love a cup of tea
It really pleases me
I sit in my room at night
And oh boy, what a sight
To see my mum bringing in
That hot, steaming mug for me.

Sarah Addis (11)
All Children's Integrated Primary School

BEACH

I walk down to the beach
To see the waves rolling
And feel the sand sliding through my fingers
As I sit and watch
The sea glistening in the sun

I walk along the promenade
And see the kids play
Throwing rocks into the sea
And burying themselves in the sand
And playing football on dry land

I watch the kids
To see if they'll ask me to come and play
Because of this beautiful day
That makes you quite hot
I need something to cool me down

As I drink my juice
I feel I'm cooling down
Very, very slowly
But I'm too tired to play
On that summer's day.

Alex Henry (10)
All Children's Integrated Primary School

HULLABALOO!

Here I come, Hullabaloo!
You can't run, Hullabaloo!
But you can hide
But I will find you
I will get you Hullabaloo!
You can catch a plane to Peru

But I will get you, Hullabaloo!
You can run to Japan
But I will catch you, I know I can
So here I come to get you
For one and all, so here I come
Hullabaloo!

Nicola Strain (11)
All Children's Integrated Primary School

HULLABALOO

I wandered through the theme park,
With the smell of chips in the air,
I looked around for a roller coaster,
So I went on and then . . .

I found it, tall as a hotel,
Glistening high in the sky,
I queued for at least two hours,
Finally I was getting on and away we went.

We shot as fast as a bullet,
Then suddenly we stopped in a steep slant,
We shot off again but this time we
Went straight downwards and into the darkness.

We went round in twists and turns,
Then there was a loop-the-loop,
There was rock music blasting in your ears,
As you went along.

Everyone was screaming
And we all darted around,
The air was flying in your face
Then finally we stopped and I walked home.

Alexi Akkari (10)
All Children's Integrated Primary School

MY TOWN

So blue the sea
Against the soft and silvery sand
The beach is quiet today
Just you and me
If it were summer, the promenade might have a band
Or a karaoke that would burst your ears
Whilst the dads go up to Diamond Pat's for beers

So blue the sea
Against the soft and silvery sand
Mum says, 'Look, I've got a pound coin in my hand,'
I jumped for joy
I knew she'd take me to the Strand
Ice cream, blue and pink, yellow, white and green
Most colours that you've ever seen
I get a great big 99

So blue the sea
Against the soft and silvery sand
The sun is shining now
Shoppers in the main street getting fewer
The mountains slowly getting bluer
Time to go
But we'll be back tomorrow.

Margaret Rogan (10)
All Children's Integrated Primary School

A SPECIAL FRIEND

A friend is someone you can trust
A friend is someone you can share you secrets with
You can help this person when they're down
And they can help you

A friend is someone you can put your faith in
And rely on
I have a special friend
And that's my dog, *Buff!*

Stewart Hanna (10)
All Children's Integrated Primary School

THE DARK

It is dark, it is not light,
It is black, it is not white,
Nothing can stop it,
Changing daytime into night.

It lurks in the corners,
When the lights are off,
Some think it's hard,
Some think it's soft.

It creeps into every crack,
It fills every hole
And under the ground,
It follows a mole.

It falls in the evening,
When everything is still,
The birds stop singing,
It brings on a chill.

But then comes the light,
Which is cheerful and bright,
Puts a smile on my face,
What a wonderful sight.

Caolann Fitzpatrick (11)
All Children's Integrated Primary School

TAKE CARE

Clean your teeth front and back
Or you'll have something called plaque
'My teeth are OK, they're not bad!'
Now looking back I wish I had.

For that night I had a terrible dream
I woke up crying and started to scream
Slimy green plaque shouting, 'Come with me.'
Toothpaste and dental floss shouting, 'Don't listen to he.'

Stuck in the middle, don't know where to go
Good or evil, I don't know
I woke in vain, my teeth were in pain.

From that day, I brushed my teeth twice a day
Like the dentist did say
I've changed my ways and I brush at night
Now my teeth are such a delight!

Kate Best (10)
All Children's Integrated Primary School

SWEETS

Sweets are juicy
Sweets are nice
Sweets are fruity
And just the right price

All different colours
On the shop shelf
It doesn't please mothers
But I'll please myself

50p in my pocket
Which will I choose?
Cola bottle or rockets?
My mum will blow a fuse

They're bad for my teeth
They're bad for my tum
But watch out Keith
'Cause here I come.

Kirsty McComish (10)
All Children's Integrated Primary School

COMPUTERS

I find it hard to think sometimes
I find it hard to work
And feel I am in a stupor
But when I sit in the classroom
I love to play the computer
Some computers are used in school
And some computers are used for work
I even saw a computer in the swimming pool
And I have one in my room
My computer is called PlayStation 2
And I love to play my games
Do you have a computer too
And has it got a name?
It is a nice toy to keep
But my mum has come in
And said, 'Time to sleep!'

Nathan Cox (10)
All Children's Integrated Primary School

CATS AND DOGS

There are lots of pets
And that's a fact
But my favourite animal
Is my pet cat
My pet cat is called Posh
And she is black and white
She is so cute
And she does not bite

I also have two dogs
One is the colour of a log
And one is black and white too
One is called Snoopdog
One is called Rio
My dogs are so small
You wouldn't notice Snoopdog if
He was stood against a wall

I wouldn't take them back
Because they both belong to me
Posh sleeps all day
So does Rio
Snoopdog just wants to play
And I just want to watch telly or listen to Nelly
I love my pets and that is true
I wouldn't swap them for anything
Even if it was new!

Laura Waddingham (10)
All Children's Integrated Primary School

SPICE

I have a cat
His name is Spice
Sometimes he's an imp
But, sometimes he's nice

He could be an angel
He could be a devil
It just depends
What's his level

He could be annoying
He could be a pest
But in the end he's
The best.

Shannin Faulkner (11)
All Children's Integrated Primary School

DENIM

Hats and bags are small accessories,
Jeans and jackets are necessities,
Blue and black is the range today,
Wear it or else you'll pay.

Purses, belts and skirts too,
Denim things are really for you,
They were in, in the 70s and they're still in,
Put all your other clothes in the bin.

Baggy, flarey, tight as well,
They're so fine, they ring a bell.
Denim comes in all shapes and sizes,
Try it on and you will get lots of surprises.

Rosie Harkness (11)
All Children's Integrated Primary School

THE FUNFAIR

T he sweet smell of candyfloss drifting in the air
H urry to the ride, feel the wind go through your hair
E verybody screaming as the ride goes upside-down

F eel the small seat, all lumpy and brown
U nderneath my seat I found a teddy someone won
N obody can see me so I'm going to take it home
F eeling very dizzy now, the ride goes round and round
A m feeling very sick now
I t's time to go, I've had a great day
R unning through the town, dizzy all the way.

Dawn Goodman (10)
All Children's Integrated Primary School

FUNFAIRS

We're going to the funfair
We're travelling by car
I think it's near the park
It seems it's really far

We pull up at the funfair
We do the ghost train first
Yuk! Look! It's only half a maid
Look behind! Gran looks afraid

A ghost pops up, a headless man
This is really scaring Gran
We leave Gran with Mum and Dad
The rest of the rides are really mad

Once we've been on all the rides
We have to go, it's closing time
I want to go again, but Gran doesn't!

Mitchell Johnson (11)
Ballyvester Primary School

HULLABALOO

Going to the airport
I'm on my holidays
Traffic jam
Too long, too far
It's getting too hot in this car!

Park the car
Haul the cases
It's always busy in these places

Push and shove
Where's the queue?
I need the loo

The plane's delayed
Six hours behind
I'm losing my mind

What a *hullabaloo!*

Emma Currie (10)
Ballyvester Primary School

POETRY

I can't think of a poem
It's really, really tough
I've only got five minutes left
And that is not enough
Nothing's coming into my brain
I think I'm going to go insane
Thank goodness now I'm nearly done
Actually this was quite fun!

Jamie Jackson (11)
Ballyvester Primary School

I LOVE FUNFAIRS

I love funfairs and cuddly bears
I like rides and slides
Pay a pound, go on the merry-go-round

Hot dogs, burger buns, fish and chips
So much fun
Toffee apples, sweets 'n' stuff, candyfloss
That's enough
Roller-coaster, Ferris wheel, I don't think I'll eat my meal

Going home on the bus
Everyone's making a big fuss
What a day!

Lauren Ramsey (11)
Ballyvester Primary School

11-PLUS

11-plus, 11-plus
What a fuss, what a fuss
All the class, all the class
Gotta pass, gotta pass
Stay calm, stay calm
Sore palm, sore palm
From writing, from writing
How exciting, how exciting!

Rachel Johnston (10)
Ballyvester Primary School

THE DELICIOUS BREW

Witches use cauldrons,
To mix up their brew.
Wizards use cauldrons,
To make a fine stew.
The immortal witch made
A celebratory trade.

Her cauldron was black
And could withstand an attack;
Of red dragon scales
And pink warthog tails,
Mixed with snake venom
And sheep guts and lemon.

Stir the pot once,
Stir the pot twice.
Whisper the spell
And check out the smell.
Leave overnight
And it'll be alright.

In the morning,
Without any warning,
The potion of slime,
Will smell like dog-breath and lime.
Ready for the rough ladle
And brought to the ceremonial table.

They come down from the highlands,
They come up from the lowlands.
Looking their best
And needing a rest.
The Dark Lord's downfall
Began this traditional ball.

Timmy Hamley (10)
Cedar Integrated Primary School

LORD OF THE RINGS

Lord of the Rings is a frightening film
Though some don't think so,
See Gollum's eyes glow in the darkness
Bet that sends a tingle up your toe,
The ring wraiths squeal
The orks roar like mad
Saruman's mind is of metal and steel
Aragorn, fearless and brave
Legolas, an expert with a bow
Gimli is below the height of men
The servants of Sauron are middle-earth's foe,
'Pack your valuables,' shouts the king's guard,
'For we flee to the refuge of Helm's Deep.'
The Uruk-Hai attack
The children are sheltered in the keep
The beserker blows up the defences
The soldiers flee and run
The Uruk-Hai chase them
Gandalf the White appears to them
For the orks are blinded by the sun.

James Steen (10)
Cedar Integrated Primary School

MY PONY

I have a pony with a silver mane,
She is white, with gold hooves.
Her name is Gold Star, Gold Star has a gold tail,
When I'm on her back and she canters,
I feel like I'm flying,

She is wonderful!
I have a pony with a silver mane,
I ride her in the sunshine,
I ride her in the rain
And I sleep in her lovely mane!

Ines Mathieu (10)
Cedar Integrated Primary School

HORSES

My friend, Anna has a horse,
Her name is Maple.
Her favourite food is apples,
Fresh from her basket in the stable.
Her mane and tail are tatty,
But her legs are strong, slender, not fatty.

Unlike David's horse, his name is Fred,
But you'll never guess he only likes bread.
He goes wild when he sees the colour orange,
What do you think? He's got no courage.
Will, his coat is black and white,
Pushed into his stable real tight.
His mane's is in tufts and tots,
He's white with black spots.

Fred's friend, Harry's horse, she's called Apple,
I suppose she likes apple crumble.
She likes running in circles round
And loves to jump and make a strange sound.
After her dinner, she drinks milk in two great gulps,
Then she runs off in two big hops
And all of a sudden she just flops.

Rebekka Hamilton (9)
Cedar Integrated Primary School

THE MONKEY POEM

He swung through the trees like Tarzan,
Making his way to the banana tree,
He swung with grace,
As his strong arms unveiled his muscles and his hands
Clenched to the branches
To stop him from falling
As he stretched to the next tree
He looked towards the ground
To see danger.
The king of the jungle roamed below
He let out a mighty growl
The monkey screeched to warn his friends and steadied
Himself on a branch, hoping to stay in the trees.
After a period of stillness
The danger passed and he was able to continue his journey
The monkey swung until he finally reached his destination -
The banana tree.

Andrew McMaster (9)
Cedar Integrated Primary School

DREAM DOG

I wish to have a dog someday,
To throw it sticks and let it play.

Bath time with it would be fun,
When it showers me before it runs.

I'd brush its coat from head to tail,
My wish would then seem so real.

Someday soon I hope to get
My dream dog if only I'm let.

Patrick Ward (9)
Cedar Integrated Primary School

THE MOURNES

Lovely Mournes resting by the sea,
A peaceful place, a place I like to be.
Bignian, Bernagh, Commedagh and Doan,
A place that no one will ever own.
I love to walk the rough and stony paths,
With my family having a lot of laughs.
The Annalong Wood is a magical place,
Where my brother and I climb trees and chase.
Noodles and ravioli are my favourite food,
Because when you're in the mountains
Anything tastes good!
Round the campfire as the sun sinks low,
A cup of tea and off to bed we go.
I wake in the morning and listen to the trickling stream,
Scratch my eyes at the early sun's beam.
Packed up,
It's sad to leave,
But we'll be back, I can definitely believe.

Alex Johnson (10)
Cedar Integrated Primary School

SNOW, SNOW

Snow, snow, when will you come,
So I can go out and have some fun?
Wrap up warm in scarf and hat,
Go whizzing down the hill on my plastic mat.

In the morning, there it is,
Better go and get my little sis.
Call for our friends to come out and play,
We'll build a snowman and have a great day.

Aidan McGrory (10)
Cedar Integrated Primary School

SCHOOL YEAR

When the school year starts
Work is easy and there isn't much to do.
Workbooks are shiny,
Handwriting is neat with dates
And underlined titles, just like
A new piece of chewing gum
Fruity and soft with
Lots of flavour.
But as the year wears on
Handwriting gets spidery,
The date is forgotten,
Work gets harder, and
The workbooks get furry,
Dog-eared and dull,
An old piece of chewing gum
Tough as leather with
Faded flavour, tasting like
All other well-chewed gum,
Whether it started as strawberry
Or peppermint or aniseed.
Eventually the year is over,
You can rest your jaws and
Take the year out of your mouth,
Put it behind you and
Move on to working hard on
A new piece of chewing gum.

Adam Mullan (10)
Cedar Integrated Primary School

SCHOOL DAYS IN THE PLAYGROUND

I walk into the playground and look all around,
Lots and lots of children playing, to be found.
Children who are happy, children who are sad,
Some of them seem very good - some very bad.
I hear the well-off children boasting about what they have,
There are others who don't have as much but seem just as glad.

Boys and girls separate when they are at play,
When the girls are skipping the boys tell them, 'Go away.'
Yet the boys never tire of football every single day.
There have been many advances through the ages,
With new schools and their rules,
But when I talk to old folk they just smile and say,
'Enjoy your days at school before they pass away.'

Alexandra Kelly (9)
Cedar Integrated Primary School

SOUNDS OF WINTER

It's cold in winter
Jack Frost is here
Hands like ice
Snowball fights
Snow on the walls
It still falls
Winter nips
Your nose
Your toes
Stay in bed
Until it goes.

Searcha Roissetter (8)
Christ The King Primary School

A WINTER POEM

If you take a look around
All you will see is snow on the ground

All the children shout hurrah
Because they are so happy today

The snow is deep, it hid the mat
Look, I can see some footprints from the cat

You really can't see anything at all
Only some snow upon the wall

All the children go out to play
But then it starts to melt away

All the children are so sad
I know what will make them glad

What was that? I heard some snow
All the children are ready to go

All the children go out to see
What that quiet noise could be

It's snow the children shout hurrah
The children are so happy today.

Shannen McCusker (8)
Christ The King Primary School

SOUNDS OF WINTER

Trees rustling in the wind
Badgers curled up underground
Children's feet crunching in the snow.

Jamie Hanna (7)
Christ The King Primary School

MY WINTER POEM

Look at the snow, all icy and white,
Let's all take our sleds and go,
Up the hill we walk,
Slow and drag our sleds in the snow,
At the top of the hill we let go,
That like the wind we go, go, go,
So summers may come
And summers may go,
But best of all, we like the snow.

Jason Savage (8)
Christ The King Primary School

THE WIND BLOWS HIGH

The wind blows high as the days go by
I saw you taking my kite
Doing robbery in daylight
Why can't I see you?
I just walk around the corner and you are in my face.
Rain, hail, sleet or snow
It all seems worse when the wind starts to blow.

Michelle O'Hare (10)
Christ The King Primary School

FROG

Green, slimy
Lives in swamps
Croaks loudly all day
Yuk!

Jamie Dougherty (9)
Christ The King Primary School

BUFFY, THE VAMPIRE SLAYER

Buffy is the slayer
She is the chosen one
Her and the Scooby gang are gonna have some fun
By day they have to go to school
By night that's when vampire are fools
Because round the corner Buffy rules
Xander, Willow, Anya and Tara are all part of the crew
Dawn and Spike help out too
She has a stake, holy water and crosses
So you better not think that you're the bosses
All you vampires and demons beware
'Cause round the corner Buffy will be there
If you think this tale's a fake
Why don't you feel the end of her stake?

Louise Lavery (11)
Christ The King Primary School

IT'S TIME TO COME IN

It's time to come in
It's time to stop the laughter and din
Put down the ball, put down the bat
Take off your gloves, take off your hat
It's time to wash, brush hair and clean
For soon we'll be sleeping, lost in a dream
Mum calls from the bathroom, your bath is ready
Walk, don't run, take it slow and steady
We kiss Mum goodnight and climb into bed
And out of sight goes our sleepy head.

Kim & Sue Dinsdale (11)
Christ The King Primary School

SCHOOL

I get up early every morning
And go down the stairs yawning
Off to school for another day
I wish I could stay at home and play

The bell rings out at 9 o'clock
The children hurry to beat the clock
I go into the class and sit on my chair
And wait for the teacher to say the prayer

Reading and writing all day long
I feel like singing a song
Too much work, not enough play
I'll have to hope for another day

The teacher says it's time to go home
And make sure all homework is done
The children all run for the bus
I don't know why they make such a fuss.

Lauren Boyd (11)
Christ The King Primary School

SPRING

Spring is when the lambs are born,
Spring is when the flowers bloom,
In spring the grass gets greener
And the chicks hatch from their eggs.
Spring makes the days grow longer,
Spring is the start of a new year,
It puts a smile on everybody's face,
Spring is the best season ever.

Shane Melville (10)
Christ The King Primary School

MY WINTER POEM

Last night I had a snow fight
I got hurt and I started to cry
And all my friends shouted, 'Lauren, bye, bye, bye'
We were playing in the fields
They were all white
And all my friends started to have a big snow fight
I was sliding down the hill
And I was freezing, so I got a chill
The snow was melting
And I was throwing snowballs
I went to throw one at my friend
And then my daddy calls
Everywhere I go my mummy will know
Because you can see my footprints all
In one row.

Lauren Morgan (9)
Christ The King Primary School

SOUNDS OF WINTER

The sound of children
Playing in the snow
Trees blowing
As the wind blows
Children throwing snowballs at each other
Sliding on the ice
Lots of snow falling
A white roof on my house
Birds flying in the white sky
Winter is here.

Ashleigh Madine (8)
Christ The King Primary School

MY DOG, BEN

My dog, Ben and I
Went out for a run
He started bouncing and jumping
We had a lot of fun
When we were finished
And could run no more
We headed back home
And were glad to see our door.

Cathy McCormick (11)
Christ The King Primary School

FOOTBALL

The team was beaming with joy,
The ref blew his whistle and it started,
I kicked the ball up and a tall boy
Headed it in the net and before the match
I made a bet,
A boy pulled my strip and it made a rip,
We won and I got some money to buy some honey.

Gary Murdock (10)
Christ The King Primary School

SOUNDS OF WINTER

Snow falls from the sky
The children yap when they fall
Dogs growl at night
Cats yap on a snowy day
Cars skidding on the road
Trees swaying in the wind.

Darren Morgan (8)
Christ The King Primary School

MY PONY

Over the hills and far away
My pony and I go out to play
My pony is fast when I use the whip
So fast, you'd think she is starting to skip

My pony is over thirteen hands in height
When she takes off, she'd give you a fright
Over the hills and up the lane
So fast, the wind it wrecks her mane

She's very gentle, caring and kind
So the dirty work I do not mind
Cleaning her stable is a smelly old chore
I say, 'Oh! Amber please no more!'

I make her bed every night
It really is a pleasant sight
To see her sleep so peaceful at last
Who would think she could move so fast.

Ashley McConville (10)
Christ The King Primary School

SOUNDS OF WINTER

The wind whistling through the park,
The snow falls softly down,
Ice cracking,
The badgers snoring underground,
Winter is here.

Nathan Madine (8)
Christ The King Primary School

WINTER'S DAY

On the winter's day the snowman did say
it's wintertime so let's play

All the boys and girls came out when it was nice and bright
and had a snowball fight.

All the roads were soon salted and then the snow was soon melted.

The children began to pray and say I wish it would snow again today.

On the winter night it began to snow, so now I know it's surely
wintertime.

A boy built a snowman with his brother, Sam.

Maria Melville (9)
Christ The King Primary School

SOUNDS OF WINTER

The kids shouting in the snow,
Kids skidding on the ice,
Dogs barking,
Cars sliding on the ice,
Cats miaowing by the night sky,
People playing on their sleigh,
Wolves howling by the moon,
Noses red, ears frozen,
Toes frozen like my nose,
People throwing snowballs,
It hits my nose.

John Cowan (8)
Christ The King Primary School

WINTER'S POEM

On a cold, chilly winter's day I ran outside to go and play,
The snow was soft under my feet but I had to hurry,
I had friends to meet.
The snow was lying on the ground,
It was everywhere when you looked around.
I looked like a big ball of cotton wool, I thought it looked cool.
I ran to the top of the big hill and the wind was blowing a big chill.
I went down the hill on my sledge,
I didn't get stopped and went into a hedge.
We built a snowman and put in stones for eyes
And had a snowball fight till the end of the day.
It was time to go home, the ground was slippery,
Everywhere was sparkling bright.
It was getting dark and it would soon be night.

Declan Byrne (8)
Christ The King Primary School

SOUNDS OF WINTER

Teeth chattering in the cold
Hands like ice
Hands rubbing together
People sitting beside the fire
Wind whistling, children laughing
People shivering
People in bed
Badgers sleeping in bed
Dogs howling
Cats hissing
Winter is here.

Patrick McAlister (7)
Christ The King Primary School

A WINTER'S DAY

Snow is falling on the ground
All the children are playing around

The children are so happy today
They don't want it to go away

In the night
You'll need to tuck in tight

All the children are making snowmen
All the men think it's them

All the children are tucked up tight
In hats and gloves so they will keep out frostbite

Anywhere you go your mum will always know
By the footprints in the snow.

Nicola Rice (9)
Christ The King Primary School

CHRISTMAS

It's now Christmas holiday time
It is my favourite season
When we all get presents
And laugh without reason
We have plenty of treats
And a big dinner
Followed by sweets
That will not make us no thinner.

Gary McCormick (11)
Christ The King Primary School

A WINTER'S DAY

One winter's day, I went out to play
Then I saw a white shape
So I put on my cape and got quietly into my PJs

I went up to bed, to rest my weary head
But was awoken by the sound of a snowman

As he danced and he danced
I didn't watch, but I glanced
As he sat down with a bump on the ground

The big lump, he did flump
As he was very plump and the sun turned him into a snowball

He then turned into a bunny and he looked very funny
And I gave out a jolly big laugh.

Michael Ritchie (8)
Christ The King Primary School

SOUNDS OF WINTER

Leaves swaying up and down,
Trees whistling in the wind,
Teeth chattering,
The crunch of children's feet on the snow,
Children's coats fastening up,
Hands shivering just like ice,
Children yelling,
Winter's here.

Amie Savage (8)
Christ The King Primary School

SOUNDS OF WINTER

Dogs howling
Cats whining
People frozen
Stiff as ice
Wind whistling
Through the trees
Bees sleeping
In their hives
Clouds black
In the sky
Rain splashing
In wintertime.

Conor Melville (8)
Christ The King Primary School

SOUNDS OF WINTER

The whirling wind blows my hat,
I break the ice with my bat,
My daddy pats corn,
He got stung by a very snowy thorn,
I sing Jingle Bells,
My daddy yells,
I fell down a hill with a bang,
'Aargh!' my daddy sang,
I went to a snowy holiday house,
With a mouse.

John Wilson (7)
Christ The King Primary School

MY WINTER POEM

One day I went outside in the back field
And saw lots of snow on the trees.
You cannot see the grass, it is all white
And I made snow angels in the night.
Last night I had a snow fight
And in the morning it was bright.
Yesterday my mummy slipped on the road
And when I went shopping I had to key in a code.
I slid on the hill
And then I got a chill
And everywhere I go
My mummy will know.
One night it was snowing
And my daddy was in bed snoring.

Stacie Sloan (9)
Christ The King Primary School

SOUNDS OF WINTER

I can hear
The snow falling softly
The sea crashing against the rocks
The wind whistling loudly
My nose is cold and red
I will stay in bed.

Shannon O'Hare (8)
Christ The King Primary School

SOUNDS OF WINTER

Snow falling softly
On the garden wall
Badgers snoring underground
Children laughing, shrieking, yelling
While they play
Crunching the snow with their feet
On a snowy day
The wind shakes
Trees, fences, grass
On a winter's day
Cars skid on the slippery ice
That makes them crash
On a winter's day.

Catriona McEvoy (8)
Christ The King Primary School

A WINTER'S DAY

One snowy day I went out to play on a cold winter's day
In the fields of pillow-soft snow,
Where the snow lay thickly on the white ground below
Where there's a crunchy sound from your footprints in the fields
Where the snowflakes drop to the ground below.
The glittering soft white snow with the slippery ice on the ground
The car slid on the ice causing everyone to look at the frosted car.

Paul Gilchrist (8)
Christ The King Primary School

A WINTER POEM

The snow is falling on the ground,
Everyone is playing around,
People's footprints in the snow,
Mummy knows where children go,
Making snow angels in the snow,
Covering ourselves as we go.

Fiona Morgan (8)
Christ The King Primary School

SOUNDS OF WINTER

In winter the leaves
Fall off the trees
The bees lie in their beds
Resting their little heads
The snow is cold in your hands.

Chelsea Russell (7)
Christ The King Primary School

ON A WINTER'S NIGHT

Snowy it was on a winter's night, my footprints were deep and bright
My friend was sliding on the ice on a winter's night
Then I saw the snowman he built in surprise on a winter's night
The snowman was perfect, he was sparkling bright on a winter's night.

Stephen Robinson (8)
Christ The King Primary School

THE ALIEN

I met an alien
Down at the shop,
But I didn't
Scream, yell or hop.

He looked like
A big bowl of jelly
And he had a
Big, round belly.

He had square eyes
And I don't tell lies,
He was short, fat and had a grin,
He said to me he lived in a bin.

He was really weird
And had a beard,
He had no ears
And he didn't cry tears.

He had some hair
And was the
Size of a
Baby bear.

I met an alien
Down at the shop,
But I didn't
Scream, yell or hop.

Bridgette Fitzsimons (10)
Convent Of Mercy Primary School

WHICH WITCH?

Winter witch
She spreads the snow
All white and glistening
Over our toes
Nobody knows where she goes
Which witch?
Summer witch
She likes the mice
Yeah right!
She wants them to
Make spells at night
They scamper and scatter
And clamper and clatter
Which witch?
Autumn witch
She gathers leaves all
Golden and brown
And tosses them up
From the dusty ground
Which witch?
Spring witch
She is tall with
Skinny, long legs
Her sharp set eyes prod our
Minds and frighten all
The earthly souls
Which witch is for you?

Hannah O'Neill (11)
Convent Of Mercy Primary School

MY BROTHER

My brother is mad about football,
He plays it every day,
In rain, snow or sun,
He always has fun,
Scoring lots of goals on the way!

Every Sunday he plays for Shamrock's FC,
To Dunleath Park we all must go,
Where we cheer on the best defender,
Who's my brother . . . in case you didn't know.

So Michael Owen watch out,
For Jordan's about
And your crown he'll surely claim.
With a boot and a header,
He'll definitely get better
And be king of *the beautiful game.*

Lyndsay Curran (11)
Convent Of Mercy Primary School

MY CLASS

Writers, fighters
Whiz kids
Choir kids
Trouble makers
Bossy boots
Mathematics fanatics
History freaks
Busy beaks
Silent sneaks
Good grief
What a week!

Kirstin Murray (10)
Convent Of Mercy Primary School

COUNTDOWN TO CHRISTMAS

Twelve days to go
Cleaning, shopping, singing

Eleven days to go
Dancing, cleaning, shopping

Ten days to go
Writing, wrapping, sending

Nine days to go
Drawing, buying, sending

Eight days to go
Hoping, washing, dusting

Seven days to go
Wishing, wondering, wrapping

Six days to go
Excited, thinking, singing

Five days to go
Buying, wrapping, wishing

Four days to go
Writing, posting, sleeping

Three days to go
Dancing, singing, sending

Two days to go
Bathing, drying, brushing

One day to go
Cooking, sleeping, singing

Christmas Day
Opening, looking, praying,
Playing, eating, resting.

Ciara Lennon (10)
Convent Of Mercy Primary School

MY CALCULATOR

Great fighters
Neat writers
Funny ones
Grumpy ones
All very
Different sums
Add if
You think
I'm mad
Distract me
If you
Want to
Subtract me
Multiply and
You can
Buy me
For 50p
Sale now on!
Divide by
2 what
Great value
I am
To you.

Sarah McStravick (11)
Convent Of Mercy Primary School

BEST FRIENDS

Best friends forever
Best friends together
Best friends we'll always be
Never part shall we
My best friend and me
Never, ever, ever

Best friends forever
Best friends together
Best friends we'll always be
Best friends together, forever and ever
You'll never see us part
Because we're very close at heart
And we're the bestest best friends there can be.

Ciara McCartan (11)
Convent Of Mercy Primary School

MY CLASS

Ruling rulers
    Maths droolers
        Copy cats
    Reading rats
Cheeky brats
    Class mates
        They're great
                Trouble makers
            Heart breakers
        3 o'clock
On the dot
            home time
    Cheery chime.

Anna Rea (11)
Convent Of Mercy Primary School

OUR MICE

We have little mice
And they're not very nice,
When they have parties,
They're very, very noisy,
They rattle our floorboards at night,
They don't like it when we turn on the light.

We have noisy mice
And they're not very nice,
The part about them I hate,
Is when they tap their feet,
When the floorboards jump,
I always get a bump.

Our little noisy mice,
They love their cheese!

Kerryanne Rhodes (11)
Convent Of Mercy Primary School

MY FRIEND

My friend is nice and kind
She is cool in the mind
Sometimes she is like a P2 or maybe P1
But she helps me all the time
We fight all the time
But in our hearts
We are best friends
I'd rather say her name
And tell you her game
Anneliese is her name
And friend is her game.

Ann-Marie McCoubrey (11)
Convent Of Mercy Primary School

THE MAN FROM CORK

The man from Cork
Who has a big fork
Would really like to visit York
Although he can't
He really might
But he wonders what to do
He says to fork, 'What will we do?'
Fork just nodded and turned away, then he said,
'Oh my dear, I have an idea.'
'Oh really, what might it be?'
'To visit York this winter, fork.'
'Oh really?'
'Yes,' he said to me.

Grainne Ritchie (10)
Convent Of Mercy Primary School

MY BABY BROTHER

Bottle biter
Dummy dropper
Cot lazy
Really crazy
Little crier
Big liar
Can crawl and
Play with a ball
I wish I could smother
My baby brother.

Terri-Louise McCarthy (10)
Convent Of Mercy Primary School

MY SISTER

She speeds like a whiz
To work and back
Her hair's in a frizz
She says, 'What's the craic?'

She's never on time
She's always late
Things would be fine
But she just can't wait

For Mr Right to come along
But it's never right, it's always wrong
Everyone tells her, 'Mr Right will come some day.'
But that will be a long, long time away.

Stephanie Hanna (10)
Convent Of Mercy Primary School

I WONDER

I sit up in my bedroom
And wonder what, what, what
It will be.
1st, 2nd, 3rd, 4th, it's not here yet,
The 8th I bet.
5th, 6th, 7th, 8th,
It is not too late.
The scene is set,
For the baby to come home,
Yet, yet, yet.

Cara Cunningham (10)
Convent Of Mercy Primary School

BUTTERFLY

Butterfly, butterfly
You fly so high
Butterfly, butterfly
Why, oh why?
With all your colours
So bright and gay
Butterfly, butterfly
Up and away.

Leanne Brady (11)
Convent Of Mercy Primary School

I WANT TO BE FREE

I want to be free said the girl to her mind,
I want to be free, to have no rules of any kind.
I want to be like a fish swimming in an open sea,
That's the only thing that I want, I want to be free.
I want to be free, like a bird in the sky,
Who could flutter and flap for mile after mile.

Andrea McCarthy (10)
Convent Of Mercy Primary School

ANOTHER YEAR

Another year has come to an end
One in which I met a new pen friend
We met in Tunisia which was grand
But not as cool as Santa in Lapland

My parents didn't make a fuss
Coz they knew I worked hard for my 11-plus
They bought me a phone for all my studies
So now I can text and phone all my buddies.

Emma Crawford (10)
Convent Of Mercy Primary School

MY SISTER

Toy hugger
   Dog lover
Bottle drinker
   Nappy stinker
Dummy sucker
   Head bumper
Bed hater
   Monster eater
Tubby lover
   Under cover.

Rachel Bogues (10)
Convent Of Mercy Primary School

THE RACES

This little boy went to the races
Even though he's too young for such places
Now he's all sad 'cause his dad is real mad
And his eyes are full of salt traces

Off to school you silly little fool
And don't try and fool me
Again!

Lauren Polly (10)
Convent Of Mercy Primary School

THE DIET

My mummy does some exercises,
To try to make her thin,
But I just sit and laugh at her
Because she keeps on giving in.

She jogs along the beach sometimes,
To try to lose some weight,
But I think she'd be better
Using a smaller plate.

She stands upon the bathroom scales
And gives a loud hurray
Because after all her hard work
Some fat has gone away.

Ciara Currie (10)
Convent Of Mercy Primary School

BUSY BEES

Busy bees flying around
They make such a buzzing sound
Carrying honey from flower to flower
And it goes on, hour by hour
Busily they go, singing their song
While doing their work which takes so long
Then they take it to the queen
Whose yellow stripes shine like beams
After work they fly back home
To their yellow house, the honeycomb.

Lisa McGrady (11)
Convent Of Mercy Primary School

MY FRIEND PAUPER

Carrot lover
Real hugger
Outside hopper
We call him Pauper
Real fluffy
He's a Duffy
Floppy ears he has
No fears
My friend, Pauper.

Tierna Duffy (11)
Convent Of Mercy Primary School

THE LIFE OF A COMPUTER

I sit in the study, on my owner's desk all day long,
Waiting patiently for them to come and switch me on,
A few clicks of my mouse and I open their files,
Sending information down the line from hundreds of miles.
Cutting and pasting and copying too,
Shortly we print a picture . . . of Winnie the Pooh!

The kids come along and pop a disc in my drive,
Hope it's dance music, I fancy a jive.
When the fun is all done and the kids go to bed,
I settle back down, *oh no a sore head!*

It's the big kids now that come over to play,
They're worse than the little ones, they stay on all day.
The mums save their recipes and chat on-line,
The dads look up fast cars most of the time!

I'm a useful little friend to have in your home,
If you haven't got one, then take my friend home.

Deborah McSpadden (8)
Crossgar Primary School

My Bedroom

My bedroom is purple and green
I share it with my sister who can be mean
She jumps on me and pulls my hair
I sometimes wish I didn't have to share

I come home from school, my bed is a mess
She really is such a pest
I do my homework
While she acts like a dork

8 o'clock and time for bed
I pull the covers over my head
'Are you sleeping yet?' I hear her say
Doesn't she know it will soon be day?

I try to ignore her questions and calls
If Mum hears her it will sound like Niagara Falls,
'Be quiet, close your eyes and get to sleep,'
Mum says 'and not another peep.'

Natalie Aimee McSpadden (10)
Crossgar Primary School

Grandparents

Old
Kind, wonderful
Buy me sweets
They love me lots
Get me things
Very funny
Grandparents.

Jenna McKeown (8)
Crossgar Primary School

THE ISLAND

Whilst on a sailing ship,
On a bumpy sea,
I crashed and tumbled out,
Oh, poor little me!

Fortunately, I could swim
And tried to swim ashore,
To a little island,
Getting closer, more and more.

I got on to the island,
Deserted and sandy,
With coconuts and bananas,
Isn't that handy!

I ate a few bananas,
They didn't taste that good,
But I should be thankful,
At least I have some food.

Oh dear, it's getting dark,
It's really very scary,
I saw some people come,
All shaggy and all hairy

They said, 'Hello, how are you?
We've lived here for ten years!'
They had hairy noses
And very heavy ears.

I think that I'll stay here,
With my brand new friends,
I'll stay with them forever,
Till the very end.

John Emerson (9)
Crossgar Primary School

TEACHERS

Teachers
Great, funny
Colouring, sums, work
Books, spellings, marking, noisy
PE, art, stories
Classes, happy
Teachers.

Kerryn Davenport (8)
Crossgar Primary School

DOGS

Very playful
Big, fat, hairy
Slow, fast, lazy, jumpy
Runny, boney, silly
Squeaky, funny
Dogs.

Sarah Coulter (7)
Crossgar Primary School

UNTITLED

Sharks
Cool, scary
Fast, attack, bad
Scared, frightened, terrified, afraid
Sharks

Dolphin
Soft, smooth
Jump, swim, eat
Wonderful, happy, excited, cheerful
Dolphin.

Kyle Strain (9)
Crossgar Primary School

WHEN I GO ON HOLIDAY

When I go on holiday
I have really good times
I go to the beach
And play in the sand and sea
But when it's time to go home
And our holiday is over
I argue with my mum and dad
That I'm staying
And then I run and run and run.

Christine Nelson (9)
Crossgar Primary School

BIRDS

Flying high
Hoping, jumping, balancing
Nice, fun, lovely, beautiful
Birds.

Ashleigh Buttle (9)
Crossgar Primary School

THE HASSLE CASTLE

Castles, castles cause loads of hassle,
The king and queen and the maid, sit and feast,
Oh, what a beast,
The king is fat, the queen is thin,
The maid is a bit of both,
Their cat is fat, oh what a fat cat,
The hassle castle has got a ghost,
A scary ghost indeed,
One dark night it came out
And scared the wits out of the king!
He jumped, he glared, he even stared,
Just like looking at e-mail post!

Jonathan Buttle (11)
Crossgar Primary School

SEASIDE

I like the seaside, it is great fun
My brothers and I lie deep down in the sun
We all like going for a paddle in the sea
Then we come back for a cup of tea
We go and lie and get a tan
Then deep in the sea we find a snorkelling man
Who is looking for fish, he has a plan
That fish will end up in his frying pan
The fish it wriggles and jiggles about
It hides deep inside and never comes out
Deep inside a treasure chest
It snuggles down and makes a nest.

Nicola McCullough (8)
Crossgar Primary School

THE SEASIDE

I like the seaside, blue and green,
That's where I like to be seen.
Swimming around, getting wet,
Catching fish in my net.
People doing lots of things,
Beautiful gannets on the wing.
Looking for fish, diving in,
I like watching the boats by,
Graceful yachts with sails set high.
Shining seashells on the sand,
I think the seaside is just grand!

Lara White (8)
Crossgar Primary School

LIFE

It's not that I suddenly don't like you or anything,
It's just that I don't know how to handle everything.
A bird's life is so simple - it must just flap a wing,
To get to where it wants - and then shall sing!
A cat can slink around and to a tree will cling,
So it may climb then purr contentedly.
Across its land a kangaroo just has to bounce
And beware of prey - that may pounce.
A wolf is not a good friend,
It will eat you up
And that will be your end!
But what about my life?
It is so complicated and hard,
It's not that I suddenly don't like you,
It's just that I don't know how to handle everything.

Caroline McEvoy (9)
Glenlola Collegiate School

PETS

Lots of people have had pets
And some die because they forget
If you forget to feed your fish
It's going to be your cat's favourite dish
If you don't clean out your horse's bed
It will be dirty for years ahead!
I have always wanted a tiger too
To prowl about the grounds with you
So if my brother bothered me
My tiger would sort him out you see!
If I had a puppy, I'd hold him so tight
And when he was older, he'd howl in the night
If I had a rabbit, it would run at my feet
And when she was good, I'd give her a treat
When animals are thinking
Well, I mean *if* they do!
What *would* they be thinking about?
The same as me and you . . .?

Lydia Collins (10)
Glenlola Collegiate School

WIND

As the wind blows through the trees
It frightens all the honeybees
The wind is strong, the wind is wild
It blows on every single child

It rustles leaves and blows them away
I love to watch them dance and play
The wind makes the waves in the deep blue sea
It blows on you and it blows on me

The wind is invisible, no eye can see
But its power is as clear as it can be
Tossing and turning
Flipping and churning
Strong and wild and free.

Sarah Blair (10)
Glenlola Collegiate School

WHERE?

There's a snowflake
Where?
Over there
Where the jungle fills the air
Where is the jungle?
Over where the sun shines bright
And the wolf howls
Wake up the moon for the night
Where's the moon?
The moon is up in the sky
That glitters when it's high
How high is high?
Think of a plane
About 30,000 feet up
Above the clouds
Where the sky is blue
But where's the snowflake?
Behind you!
Boo!

Mai Worthington (9)
Glenlola Collegiate School

THE ROOMS IN MY HOUSE

My bedroom's like a jungle
I climb through all the trees
There are so many obstacles
I don't do it with ease

My brother's room's so smelly
With rubbish shoes and clothes
He never tidies anything
The mess just grows and grows!

My parent's room is pretty
While mine is such a mess
Theirs is sugar, mine is spice
On tidiness I'd get less

The spare room is so cosy
It's my playroom with a bed
It's sugar-pink and rosy
With my favourite ted!

The front room is most comfy
With a big TV and Sky
A sofa big enough to be a bed
Oh, what a place to lie!

The toilet is the 'wee room'
It has a picture with my au pair
It brings back lots of memories
Of things we can share

The kitchen, with the oven
The washing machine and sink
The room with all the action
My mum's in there, I think!

Bryony Gray (9)
Glenlola Collegiate School

IDOLS

Westlife are simply the best.
Britney Spears has me in tears.
Kelly Osborne is above all the rest.
Zoe Birklet is a bird.
Nelly is an elephant.
Romeo is in love with Christina,
For Christina has a million bucks!
Ashanti has something for Ja Rule.
LL Cool Jay is a big slot.
Gareth Gates is very cute.
Will Young is very boring.
Rosie Ribbons has me snoring.
Eminem has a lot to learn.
Dr Dre is the best rapper!

Sophie Goddard (10)
Glenlola Collegiate School

MY FRIEND

My friend is special,
She's one of a kind.

She's like a cool breeze on a hot summer's day,
She'll cheer you up if you are sad.

If I'm sick and not feeling too well,
She'll help me get better with the ring of a bell.

She'd help me out if I got in trouble
And say it was her to blame.

She's my best friend now and has been for as long as I can remember,
We're best friends forever.

Ciara Edwards (10)
Glenlola Collegiate School

RUGBY

As we get closer to Ravenhill
I see the floodlights shining like a star in the sky
It's an hour to kick-off, the ground is buzzing
You can feel and smell the excitement in the air

We run for our seats to get the best view
Ulster runs out onto the pitch, the roar from the crowd is deafening
The game has finally started
The tackles are fast and furious, Ulster are determined to win

The shouts of 'Try! Ulster!' Along with 'Come on!'
Echo round the stadium
They take their chances and finally come out on top
The streets are full of people heading home
I look back and the floodlights go out
The excitement is over.

Ciara Lucas (10)
Glenlola Collegiate School

THE SEASIDE

My house is very near the sea
In the pretty town of Donaghadee
The waves do crash upon the shore
They'll keep on going for evermore
Our lighthouse stands at the end of the pier
Warning the ships not to come near
Our lifeboat is a famous one
It has saved many a father and son.

Ellen Warwick (11)
Glenlola Collegiate School

SNOWFLAKE

I am a small snowflake
Nobody notices me
As I slowly float down to the ground
Look closely or you won't see

I am a small snowflake
There are no two of us alike
Everyone is special
As we shine white and bright

I am a small snowflake
I fall from the sky
But now that I have reached the ground
Sadly I melt and die.

Antonia Clements (11)
Glenlola Collegiate School

MY DOG, SAM

My dog is Sam
His breed name says 'he retrieves'
But he seems to think his job is
To lie on the settee

Sam gets excited about a walk
But then he's as slow as can be
He plods along until he knows
He'll soon be back on the settee

I may say things about Sam
Which make him sound annoying
But my favourite place on a Saturday morning
Is beside him on the settee.

Kerry Adrain (11)
Glenlola Collegiate School

THE DOLPHIN

The dolphin is a blue fish, it lives in the sea
It goes in and out as it jumps up at me
It swims and it swims and it follows my boat
When I jump in the water, it helps me to float.

Hannah Sharpley (11)
Glenlola Collegiate School

MY EYES

This is the eye that can
See the blue coloured sky

This is the eye that can
See the black dark cloudy sky

This is the eye that can
Look to see a bad accident

This is the eye that can
See good things

This is the eye that can
See bad things

This is the eye that can
See the moonlit sky

This is the eye that can
See enormous things.

This is the eye.

Adam Murnin (9)
Grange Park Primary School

WHAT A POEM IS NOT

A poem is not an ant, though it can be quite short.
A poem is not a banana, though there can be something under the skin.
A poem is not a comb; so don't try to brush your hair with it.
A poem is not a drum, but it can have a beat.
A poem is not an endless pair of trousers, though it may be quite long.
A poem is not a dose of the flu, though it can be quite catching.
A poem is not a great number of things.
A poem is not a house, though it can be quite homely.
A poem is not an ice cream and I think that's a pity.
A poem is not a jumper, but it can be warm.
A poem is not a kite, but it may like the wind.
A poem is not a lullaby, though it may put you to sleep.
A poem is not a mirage, it is perfectly real.
A poem is not a nife, but it can spell words wrongly.
A poem is not an Olympic medallist; can't you see it has no legs?
A poem is not a bottomless pit, though it may be quite deep.
A poem is not a queen, nor is it a ruler.
A poem is not a radio station, though you may need to tune into it.
A poem is not a squid and I think that is quite understandable.
A poem is not a trap, and it shouldn't feel like one either.
A poem is not an umbrella, though it may give protection.
A poem is not a violin, but it can sound just as bad.
A poem is not a window, you cannot see through it.
A poem is not an x-ray; it does not need to look at your broken bones.
A poem is not a yacht, so don't send it sailing.
A poem is not a zebra, but that does not say it doesn't belong in a zoo.

Sara Ebbinghaus (11)
Grange Park Primary School

THE WOLF

The wolf he lives in the dark, dark wood
At night he hunts for his food
All day he sleeps inside his bed
Wrapped up in leaves, gold, brown and red
At night you can hear him howling
When he snores, it sounds like he's growling
He's as smelly and dirty as you could possibly be
He may even have some itchy fleas
His teeth are sharp, his claws are sore
He could be in an army in the First World War
He is as ferocious as can be
So he can hunt for food for his tea
He's vicious, ferocious, huge and he's hairy
He certainly is incredibly scary
I think he is my best, best friend
I'll love and adore him to the very end.

Katrina Wolsey (8)
Grange Park Primary School

THIS IS THE HAND

This is the hand which hugs my mummy.
This is the hand which cracks the fingers.
This is the hand which claps.
This is the hand which hits people.
This is the hand which touches wool.
This is the hand which touches mud.
This is the hand which likes to touch fluffy cats.
This is the hand which doesn't like to touch hairy spiders.

Patrick Boomer (8)
Grange Park Primary School

CATS

Cats
Some are small
Some are big
Some are playing with a ball
Some are fat
Some are skinny
But none of these
Describe my cat
You see
My cat
Plays with me
All day long
Then he's gone, fast asleep
Without a peep
And in the morning
He's ready to leap.

Adam Caughey (9)
Grange Park Primary School

MY FEET

These are the feet that jump and dance
In the brown and yellow crinkled leaves
These are the feet that sink slowly in the summer sand
Which scalds the toes and runs to the deep blue sea
Like a bottomless pit of water
These are the feet that love to leap and prance
These are the feet that crunch the snow like cotton wool
And freeze like icicles
These are the feet that run away when I get scared!

Paris Aumonier (8)
Grange Park Primary School

THE BURGLARY

Woof! Woof!
Dogs bark at the sound of a snapping branch,
They stop.
A dark figure breathes a silent 'Phew!'
He steps forward.
Silence.
The figure stands muttering to himself.
He starts his way up the trellis,
It creaks. He stops.
Snap!
He jumps.
'Phew! Made it,' comes the sigh of relief.
A body hangs silently from a window sill,
A window is opened noisily,
Only the thief hears his sole scrape the window sill.
The floorboards creak as he makes his way to the light switch.
Click,
The light clicks on,
Clang!
The thief drops the trophy he is holding,
He holds his breath,
Nothing.
He goes ahead with his dirty deed.
He stops,
Sirens!
Rubber tyres screech on the tarmac outside.
A door downstairs slams open.

'You're under arrest!' shouts a voice.
'Never!' comes the reply from the figure reaching inside his jacket,
Bang!
A gunshot,
The dark figure is no more,
His dirty deed is never accomplished.

Piers Aicken (11)
Grange Park Primary School

IMAGINE

Imagine a pig
as big as a squid

Imagine a house
as small as a mouse

Imagine a star
as big as Mars

Imagine a dolphin
as big as a coffin

Imagine a girl
as small as a pearl

Imagine a boy
as small as a toy

Imagine.

Rachel Waugh (8)
Grange Park Primary School

WEEKDAY BLUES

Monday morning
It's the start of the week
It's ages to the weekend
And everything looks bleak

Tuesday morning
And I forgot my netball things
I just can't wait
Until the bell rings

Wednesday morning
Half-way there
The car broke down
But I don't care

Thursday morning
It's PE today
And the weekend's
Just a day away

Friday morning
It's less than a day to wait
It's been so long
I'm glad weekends can't be late.

Victoria Finlay (10)
Grange Park Primary School

INSTRUMENTS

The drums rumble
The trumpet trembles
All you hear is a clatter
Clat, chat

The violin howls
All day long
The guitar twangs
Just like a boy in
A bad temper.

Peter Brown (11)
Grange Park Primary School

CREATURES IN THE DARKNESS

I am a creature, soft and brown
I run inside my warren at dawn
Through the network of soft beds
We all lie down and rest our heads

I'll protect my family from a snake
All my friends would like to shake
My paws if only they knew what I've done
To help us all and not just run

I'm related to the bunny
Most will say I'm not so funny
If I run and squeak and hide
From fierce creatures all outside

We are the creatures of the dark
We won't yowl and we won't bark
A bunny, mongoose and a shrew
Don't be scared, they're scared of *you!*

Rebekah Tipping (10)
Grange Park Primary School

MY SNAKE

My snake
Slithers all day long
Eating rats and mice
He doesn't have a care
In his life
That's my snake's life!

Sometimes he's sleepy
Sometimes he's grumpy
Sometimes he's hungry
Sometimes he bites
He is a feisty little chap

But other times he is sweet and nice.

Luke Coulter (8)
Grange Park Primary School

LIONS

Lions roaring at the sun,
Huge, ferocious, scary lions.
Eating tiny little deer in every second that you count.
Some are clean, some are dirty,
Some are strong, but some are weak and tiny.
Camouflaged for a deer to come
And before you know it,
A pounce will come.
Huge, ferocious, scary lions,
Waiting to pounce on every deer in eyesight!
Huge, ferocious, scary lions.

Peter Allen (9)
Grange Park Primary School

SPRING

Out come the flowers
Out comes the sun
Out come the lambs
Now spring has begun

Listen to the birds sing
High up in the trees
Can you hear the wind blow?
Making quite a breeze

Can you spot the daffodils?
Yellow like the sun
Everything comes to life again
Now spring has begun.

Hannah Campbell (10)
Grange Park Primary School

PLANETS

Planets in space
Don't have a face
They usually have a moon
But not any doom

They don't have any weather
Or any feathers
They orbit the sun and have some fun.

Simon Hull (9)
Grange Park Primary School

I AM

I am a plate of sausages and chips
You are
A tiny, slimy black slug
I am
A bunch of red roses
You are homework
I am
Maths
You are
English
I am
Cumberland pie
You are a brussel sprout
But I still like you anyway.

Zoë Brown (9)
Grange Park Primary School

MY HAND

This is the hand that hugs my mum when I go to sleep.
This is the hand that feels the cold white snow.
This is the hand that cuddles my baby warmly.
This is the hand that feels my mum's soft face.
This is the hand that feels the soft curtains.
This is the hand that feels the soft new carpet.

This is the hand that hates to feel slimy slugs.
This is the hand that sometimes smacks quite hard.

What would I do without my hands?

Rebecca McDowell (8)
Grange Park Primary School

I Am A Car

I am a car
I obey my boss the traffic lights
With my headlights and brakes
I zoom!
Down the motorway
Watch out!
I am a car
I race you down the motorway
I can hear you with my mirror ears
You control me with your feet
Watch out!
I am a car
I let you out after I win the race
Watch out!
I am a car.

Lydia McMullen (8)
Grange Park Primary School

Classroom Noises

I hear the teacher shouting loudly if a child gets a sum wrong

I hear chairs being dragged slowly across a polished floor

I hear chalk screeching on the blackboard

I hear crisp bags being scrunched at break time

I hear rulers being clanged off the table

And finally I hear

The crooning hum of the home time bell.

Amy Ferguson (10)
Grange Park Primary School

EYES

These are the eyes that see the light-blue sky
On a warm summer's day
These are the eyes that see the moonlit sky
On a frosty winter's night

These are the eyes that see the rabbit
As soft as a fluffy teddy bear
These are the eyes that see the elephant
As big as a bus

These are the eyes that see my mother when she's angry
When I've done something wrong
These are the eyes that see my mother when she's feeling great
That's when I'm in a good mood

These are the eyes that see everything around me.

Oliver Brown (9)
Grange Park Primary School

CLASSROOM NOISES

Some children are talking, whispering quietly,
A teacher shouts as she drags a wiper across the board.
Computer keys click and clink as they are pushed down,
Pupils are driving pens up and down their pages.
Shoes boom as they hit the hard wooden floor,
The door opens, creaks and slams as a messenger comes in.
The wind blows at the windows trying to force them open.
A ruler crashes to the ground and the chair groans as the
                                        child retrieves it.

Rachel Jones (11)
Grange Park Primary School

THE CRASH

The hum of the car getting started
The rush of the wheels on the road
The boom of the radio up full blast
Then, suddenly
The bang of the horn
The squeal of tyres skidding on the road
The topple and fall of the lorry on one side
The high-pitched scream
Of a teenager, crying over her boyfriend
Then
Worst of all
The long-lasting silence
But what I didn't hear
Was the click of a seatbelt.

Emily Allen (11)
Grange Park Primary School

SOUNDS

The kettle is singing
While the doorbell is ringing
Music blaring really loud
Makes *me* want to shout aloud
Mum is making everyone's tea
While Dad lies snoring on the settee
The television is talking
People start walking
All the sounds in the house
No one hears the mouse.

Kathryn Boyd (11)
Grange Park Primary School

LULU

Lulu is black
Black as a sack
She's a dog
You'll just see her in the fog
She's nosy
She's cosy
She's fun
And loves the sun
She's fast as lightning
So fast it is frightening
We're both fans of running
So we ran 20 miles which was stunning
Then we stopped and ate a bun
I forgot to tell you, I'm the daughter of a nun
She burst a small ball
And pushed my brother and made him fall!
She likes bouncy eggs
For food she begs
But it's time to go to bed
Lulu is just fed
As I lie asleep
There isn't a single peep
Tomorrow is another day
Then we'll go and play!

Lianne Mitchel (8)
Grange Park Primary School

MY CAT, BOOTS

A bundle of fun
That pounces and plays
A black ball of fur
With four cute white legs

A cuddly pussy cat
For me to adore
She's fluffy and friendly
And fab and much more.

Catherine Kennedy (9)
Grange Park Primary School

MY BEDROOM

My bedroom,
My bedroom is a cave of wonders,
Full of unusual treasures
And intriguing puzzles,
It can be magical and mysterious when it wants to be.

My bedroom is like the wide ocean,
There is no land or civilisation as far as the eye can see,
Except there are only two fish,
It can be deep and undiscovered when it wants to be.

My bedroom is like a dark forest,
The clothes in the wardrobe seem to shuffle around,
Like trees in a breeze,
It can be cold and lonely when it wants to be.

My bedroom is like never-ending space,
The bright light above my head being the blazing sun,
In the dark, you can almost imagine the stars and planets,
My bedroom can be open and starry when it wants to be.

My bedroom is like a doormat,
Welcoming and happy,
No matter what mood I'm in,
My bedroom can be my friend, always.

Katie Gillespie (11)
Grange Park Primary School

I AM

I am a cheeseburger
You are a slimy green toad
I am a pair of golden socks
You are grey pants
I am a killer whale
You are a goldfish
I am a bee
You are a baby wasp.

Peter Sames (8)
Grange Park Primary School

I AM, YOU ARE

I am a fresh plate of chips
You are a cold, rotten cabbage
I am a hot, shiny sun
You are a damp, cold cloud
I am a drink of Coke
You are a drop of water
But anyway, you're still my friend.

Alistair Stoops (8)
Grange Park Primary School

MY MOUTH

This is the mouth that tastes the salt in fresh sea air.
This is the mouth that tastes the food of foreign continents.
This is the mouth that goes *blah, blah, blah* all day long.
This is the mouth that tells people off.
This is the mouth that everyone wishes would just be quiet.

Owen Glenn (9)
Grange Park Primary School

SECRETS

My secrets are stored in my diary
Hidden away under my bed
My secrets are stored in my diary
Full of the thoughts that are inside my head
My secrets are stored in my diary
The diary that no one can read
My secrets are stored in my diary
My brothers will try but will never succeed!

I tell my diary everything,
Feelings, thoughts and secrets too
I tell my diary everything
Tell me this, do you?

Ashleigh McClurg (11)
Grange Park Primary School

I AM

I am a cat
You are a mouse

I am a daisy
You are a weed

I am a rice krispie bun
You are a cabbage

But I'm still your friend.

Lorna Bryson (8)
Grange Park Primary School

A PLACE I GO

The place I go to be alone,
Is a simple field near a humble home.
It has a little trickling stream,
I sit and think and watch it gleam.

The little flowers entwined in grass,
I always see 'til the summer's last.
The single tree, a mighty oak,
Gives shade to me, not other folk.

The sun beats down all the time,
This simple field is always mine.
In summer, autumn, winter, spring,
I always come to think on things.

My simple field near a humble home,
Is the place I come to be alone.

Cara Heaslip (10)
Grange Park Primary School

SOUNDS OF TRANQUILLITY

The sounds of children's laughter as they play in the sun,
The sounds of bees buzzing round the delicate flowers,
The sound of waves crashing against the sides of the boats.

The sound of children's sleighs slushing the snow as they gently
                                        glide down a steep hill,
The sound of squirrels scurrying to holes to hibernate,
The sound of the robin chirping away as winter comes and goes.

Victoria Wilson (10)
Grange Park Primary School

THESE ARE THE EARS

These are the ears which
Hear the loud crunch of
The dry leaves of autumn.
These are the ears which
Hear the gentle patter of
The raindrops like tiny
People walking in the park.
These are the ears which
Hear noisy friends like
Stampeding elephants in the jungle.
These are the ears which
Hear the deafening sound of
Thunder and lightning.
These are the ears which
Hear the scribble of pencils
In school.

John Agar (9)
Grange Park Primary School

LISTENING CAREFULLY

The fire is burning
The clock is turning
The phone is ringing
The radio is singing

The TV is flashing
The rain is lashing
The floorboards creak
I dare not speak.

Simon Brown (10)
Grange Park Primary School

SOUNDS OF THE STREET

The sounds of people laughing along the street,
Listen to the birds as they cheep, cheep, cheep.
The sound of cars driving steadily down the road,
I hear the lorries sigh as they start to unload.
Across the street I see men having a smoke
And a lady in a café drinking a Coke.
In the pub there are people chatting over a beer
And I hear the learner driver try to find first gear.
At the local garage I hear spanners clanging around,
But a few hours later,
It's night-time
And there's not a single sound.

Suzanne Hinds (10)
Grange Park Primary School

SOUNDS

In my living room there is:
the soft warm tick of the big brown clock,
the heavy thumping beat of the pop band on CD,
the shrill noisy laughter of my brother,
the slow squeaking hinge of the door closing
and the comforting crackling sound of the firewood.

James Henderson (11)
Grange Park Primary School

THE SNOWMAN

The snowman starts out as two small balls
Soon he stands up smart and tall
He needs two eyes, a mouth and nose
Then he'll be ready to stand and pose
At twelve o'clock he comes alive
He goes to the garden to see the beehive
He puts his hand inside and gets quite a sting
He jumps around and begins to sing
Soon his hand cheers up
Then he tells them they're far too abrupt!
He goes to the pool
And says it's real cool!
At six o'clock he begins to melt
All that's left is his hat made of felt!

Emma-Jayne Johnston (11)
Iveagh Primary School

A RECIPE FOR CHRISTMAS

Take a Christmas tree and decorations for it,
Take some food and sweets for after,
Add in a choir of carol singers,
With lots and lots of snow,
Mix with lots of large presents,
Get a turkey for dinner,
Put lights on the house for the Christmas party,
Put lights on the Christmas tree,
Take a cup of snow,
Add in the Three Wise Men,
And Jesus as well.

Gary Elliott (10)
Iveagh Primary School

HOPE AND FEAR

Hope:
Hope is lime-green,
It smells like hot, melted chocolate,
Hope tastes like a giant box of humbug sweeties,
It sounds like lots of children laughing happily,
It feels like a soft, furry kitten,
Hope lives in the heart.

Fear:
Fear is as black as the sky on a rainy day,
It smells like a burnt turkey on Christmas Day,
Fear tastes like a plate of really hot curry,
It sounds like a baby that won't stop crying,
It feels like hard rock that sticks in your teeth,
Fear lives in a devil.

Joanna Simpson (10)
Iveagh Primary School

PAIN AND HEALTH

Pain is deep-black
Pain smells like my mum's perfume
Pain tastes like butter beans
Pain sounds like someone screaming
Pain feels like a hot boiling volcano
Pain lives in your smart head

Health is like a light-yellow
Health smells like my dad's aftershave
Health tastes like custard in a bowl
Health sounds like someone singing
Health feels like a soft bed
Health lives in your body.

Robert Bell (10)
Iveagh Primary School

A Recipe For Christmas

Mix a dessert spoon of four sour sweets,
Stir in a handful of Christmas crackers to give it a pop,
Add a whole lot of bells and lights to ring it up,
Collect some holly and throw it in the bowl to spike it up,
Put in a pinch of snow to give it a freeze,
Pour in two cups of loving family to give it a heart,
Beat in some grams of reindeers to give it a kick,
Sprinkle three pounds of presents to have surprises,
Heat up some turkey with some wise men,
Toss in five ladles of Christmas trees and one teaspoon of
                                     singing carol singers,
Shake a lot of family and friends to give it some kindness and
                                            to make it nice!

Karl Liddiard (9)
Iveagh Primary School

Love And Hatred

Love is as pink as somebody's cheeks after being in the snow,
It smells like red roses swaying in the summer breeze,
Love tastes like the honeycomb in a Cadbury's Crunchie bar,
It feels like a silk dress ready to be worn,
Love sounds like robins and thrushes singing,
Love lives deep inside our hearts

The colour of hatred is dark like a stormy night,
Hatred smells like a scrapyard full of metal and old nappies,
It tastes like mushy, green peas and tomatoes,
Hatred sounds like screaming and moaning,
It feels like a sting from a scorpion's tail,
Hatred lives inside a witch.

Ross McKee (10)
Iveagh Primary School

A RECIPE FOR CHRISTMAS

Take a pinch of snow,
Add some ham to make it warm,
Use a shake of sweets to make it happy,
Next use a choir to make it sing,
Place some colourful lights to make it bright,
Add a dash of merry angels to make it glow,
Pour a golden star to make it shine,
Place a shiny cracker to make it snap,
Heat a juicy turkey to make it crispy,
Mix some sparkling presents to make it sparkle,
Fry some shepherds to make it joyful,
Next put in a Christmas tree to make it glitter,
Sprinkle a cheery ring to make it jolly,
Boil some bells to make it bright,
Whisk a cheery Santa to make it overjoyed,
Finally, add a family to make it just right.

Matthew Loughlin (10)
Iveagh Primary School

THE PALINDROMES

There's Mum and Dad
Dad drives a racecar
Mum does good deeds
And cooks on the Aga
Then there's baby Bob
Who wears a bib
There's Hannah and Anna, the twins
Who eat the pips out of every apple
And say 'Wow' all the time
Lil drinks lots of pop and goes hyper
Dad is obsessed with radar!

Hannah McKnight (11)
Iveagh Primary School

HOPE AND FEAR

Hope is golden
It smells like sweet honey dripping from a spoon
It tastes like a soothing cup of hot tea, on a cold day
Hope sounds like the whispering of butterflies flapping their wings
It feels wonderful like the touch of a mother's lips kissing
                                                    you goodnight
It lives way up in Heaven with the gentle angels

Fear is sapphire-blue, it smells like a rotten apple lying in the bin
It tastes like burnt toast sitting on a plate
Fear sounds like a child crying with nobody to hear it
It feels like the trigger on a shotgun
Fear lives alone underground.

Heather Bell (10)
Iveagh Primary School

HOPE AND FEAR

Hope is indigo
It smells like violets blooming in the spring breeze
It tastes like someone tasting ice cream on a hot summer's day
Hope sounds like a bird singing in the morning sky
It feels like someone wearing a silk dress
Hope lives in the middle of a rose

Fear is dark-grey
It smells of smoke coming from a bonfire
It tastes like a soggy rich tea biscuit
Fear sounds like a baby crying in bed
It feels like someone touching the hottest water in the world
Fear lives in the heart of a snake.

Sara Dougan (9)
Iveagh Primary School

A RECIPE FOR CHRISTMAS

Take 10 ounces of turkey and stuffing,
Add some shiny bells and decorations,
Mix in 3 wise men,
Cook slowly with a big Christmas tree,
Sprinkle on some icy snow.

Stephen Sloane (10)
Iveagh Primary School

JULY SCORCHER

July,
Beautiful sight
Excited children . . . wait . . .
For sunset and then barbecue
Then bed!

Joanna Simpson (11)
Iveagh Primary School

DECEMBER'S SNOW

Thrilling . . .
Frosty, white snow
To fall out of the sky
Now longing for Christmas presents . . .
Can't wait!

April Niblock (10)
Iveagh Primary School

SNOW DAYS

Short day,
Sun says goodbye,
Everyone is inside,
No more playing in the garden,
Bye, bye!

Amy Shannon (10)
Iveagh Primary School

DECEMBER DAYS

Snow falls . . .
The sky is white,
Everything is gleaming,
Snowflakes are sparkling all around,
It's cold.

Ryan Weir (11)
Iveagh Primary School

DECEMBER IS HERE!

Snow comes,
A joyful time,
You need to wrap up warm,
Contented children play outside,
Freezing!

Laura Phillips (10)
Iveagh Primary School

Up In The Attic

(And something's . . . watching)
Lots of ancient newspapers dated 1836
Heaps of dusty, pallid paintings now forgotten
A few dead mice slaughtered by the cat
A squeaky, battered bike, it's ready to fall apart
Mouldy pieces of biscuit stolen by the mice
Huge rusted, creaky chests never to be opened
Up in the attic . . .

Down in the cellar . . .
A rolled-up carpet crawling with bugs
Rickety wine racks shelved with glass
Smashed gas lamps filled with dirt
A woodworm-filled piano, its keys all broken
A bag of rat poison yet to be used
(And something's . . . lurking).

Hugo Harbinson (10)
Iveagh Primary School

Oak Tree

The roots are as thin as stick-insects creeping over soil
The trunk as tall as a giraffe's neck
The bark as rough as the ground outside
The leaves are as lobed and smooth as the lobes on your ears
The leaves are as colourful as a rainbow
The acorn is like an egg in an eggcup.

Stewart Gracey (9)
Iveagh Primary School

Up In The Attic And Down In The Cellar

Do you hear that? Something's lurking . . .
Oh look! There's my red Game Boy, is it still working?
Here, have this mouldy sweet, let's see what it can do
Try pushing this pram, it won't even move
A box full of toys, loads of diggers that would be fit
for some boys
An old doll lies, covered in worn clothes that give her a disguise
Up in the attic . . .

Down in the cellar . . .
Down in the cellar, soaked wooden wine racks
A disgusting scent of out-of-date pickles and garlic
Roams throughout the room, one quivers when entering it
My brother's cracked plaster that broke while he was playing
Wait! Can you hear that? Something's screaming!

Maeve Henry (10)
Iveagh Primary School

Summer Days

It's hot
The beach is packed
Kids playing in the sea
Parents sunbathing in the sun
So hot!

Callum Elias (11)
Iveagh Primary School

GABBY

Do you know Gabby the talking horse?
She is in my school doing a Spanish course.
She's so clumsy and so daft,
She talks to the furniture and makes everyone laugh
She talks to the clock and asks why it ticks
She talks to the dog and asks why it licks
She talks to the books and they do not reply
So she walks on past with a big loud sigh
She comes out of school and goes to the shop
She walks through the door and slips on a mop
She talks to the air all around,
'Why are you so quiet? You don't make a sound.'
The only sound she can hear
Is the sound of the wind going through her ear.
Gabby stands up and walks on home
With no one to talk to she looks all alone,
She goes into her house and goes to sleep
A few days later she hears some sheep
So she goes outside with a smile on her face
But comes back in with a frown of disgrace
The sheep all laugh with tears of joy
With all the sleep she took, she looks like a boy,
Gabby cries in her dark small room
Only with sadness and heartbreaking gloom.
One week on in summer
She started to get glummer and glummer,
In winter she was taller than the fence
She grew so tall she could sit on the bench,
A dog came along and they became good friends
Gabby was happy in the end.

Maille Beth Connolly (9)
Jonesborough Primary School

CLOCKS

Have you ever tried to concentrate
So hard your brain might burst
Well, I have, so don't try it
And clocks don't help much

The ticking of the clock
Goes on all day
Really getting on my nerves
More than you think

When I'm trying to read
Tick tock, tick tock
I just want to scream
I really hate my clock

Everywhere I go there is a clock
And every half an hour I hear
Ding dong, ding dong
So I go out to play

I go to my friend's house
And think the clock is gone
But in half an hour's time
Ding dong, ding dong

You always say your enemy
Is someone at school
But I know who mine is when I hear
Ding dong, ding dong, ding dong.

Laura Johnston (10)
Millisle Primary School

TROUBLE IN THE HOUSE!

This morning it was quiet
And everyone was in bed
Erin got up and went downstairs
Her mother heard her and said,
'Get back up here and go to sleep
I do not want to hear a peep!'
She ran downstairs and grabbed Erin's hair
Her sister, Sara and her dad heard all this fuss
They went down and said, 'That's not fair!'
'Aargh!' squealed Sara. 'Ouch!' cried Erin
Alas their neighbour barged in,
'What's the big din?'
She rang the police and said, 'Get over here,'
But they never came
Erin got tired of all the commotion
So she climbed the stairs and got into bed!
'I've caused enough trouble in the house.'
She slept as quietly as a mouse.

Hannah McNamara (9)
Millisle Primary School

STELLA AND BELLA

Stella and Bella
Were proud as could be,
They were perfect and posh
And hadn't one flea.

Stella and Bella
Couldn't be apart,
They were the best of friends,
Right from the start.

Stella and Bella
Were the coolest cats in town,
They hit the dance floor,
Noon to sundown.

Stella and Bella,
To be precise,
Became two pop stars
And ate no more mice.

Ashleigh McCullough (11)
Millisle Primary School

BRADLEY

You're the blood on my scraped knee,
You're the clown on my TV,
You're the beaches, silent all night,
You're the one who gives you light.

You're the one who makes me happy,
You're the fake fur, nice and fluffy,
You're the person who buys me Coke,
You're the one who laughs when I joke.

You're the pot noodle in the shop,
You're the one who makes me bop.
You're the hot tea in my kettle,
You're the one who makes me settle.

You're the dog I walk every day,
You're the friend until the end,
You're here with me all day,
Until it's time to go home.

Alex Sword (10)
Millisle Primary School

ANCIENT EGYPT

In ancient Egypt
Tutankhamun was buried
Some people
Were really worried

When they found the tomb
People thought they were cursed
If they took out the mummy
It would be worse!

Lord Carnarfon and Howard Carter
Were really brave men
They were the ones who found the tomb
Would they do it again?

Dale Adams (8)
Millisle Primary School

BEST FRIENDS

B   is for best, she's the best friend I have,
E   is for ever, I will be her friend forever,
S   is for special, she is so special,
T   is for teasing, I tease her a lot.

F   is for friendship, we will always be together,
R   is for ready, she is always ready to play,
I   is for illness, she sometimes is sick,
E   is for enjoy, we enjoy all our games,
N   is for naughty, it's fun to be naughty,
D   is for down, when we fall out,
S   is for surprise, which we do to each other.

Laura McGimpsey (9)
Millisle Primary School

My Nan

You're like a hot, tasty fragadilla,
You're like a tin of 7UP
Trickling down my throat.
You're like a rose in a flower shop,
You're like soft silk when I hug you.

You're fun when I come up to see you,
Like the fun I had at Pots Park.
You're like old songs I love to hear,
You're like my birthday presents,
Filled with joy when I come to see you.

Stephen Rea (11)
Millisle Primary School

Snow Queen

S is for snow, so cold and freezing
N is for my nose, because I'm always sneezing
O is for outside, where the snow lies
W is for winter, when the birds say their goodbyes

Q is for snow queen whom I would like to be
U is for under the tree, where I feel free
E is for everywhere, everywhere there's snow
E is for everyone who has a warm glow
N is for now, the time has come for everyone to have fun.

Caroline Atkinson (9)
Millisle Primary School

MY BIRTHDAY

About my birthday
I can't wait
It's making me feel sick
I feel I'm going to faint
As I lie in my bed
Hoping for money and sweets
For cards, surprises as well

As the morning sun rises
I jump out of bed and am full of excitement
I run into my mum's bed
She wakes up and says, 'Happy Birthday!'
Then I hug her and say, 'Can I have my cards now?'

Laura McAuley (9)
Millisle Primary School

THE JUNGLE

The jungle is a fierce place
There are all different things about
Like a fierce tiger or a huge lion

The jungle is a fierce place
You may even find spiders
Or a poisonous snake going hiss
Or maybe a gorilla that makes a noise like *ooo*

The jungle is a fierce place
So watch they don't bite.

Walter Newell (9)
Millisle Primary School

KATHRYN

You're a rose in my garden,
You're like the soft music, like Westlife.
You're like the smell of burger and chips,
You're Kathryn Colwell - you're kind and funny.
You're like water dripping from the tap,
You're just like my staying in bed.
You're full of the giggles
And that's the way I like you.

Alyson Mulholland (10)
Millisle Primary School

I HATE TIGERS!

Oh, I hate tigers, I hate them!
I don't know why, I just do.
One day they tore up my shorts,
I'll get them back, just you wait and see.

I can't stand in front of them a second,
They just lie around eating meat.
Everybody says they're neat,
All they are is a pain in the neck!

Lions are better than those things!
I don't know why tigers get so much attention?
I came home and my toy gun was stolen
And I automatically thought it was a tiger!

I went to the zoo and threw stones at them
And got thrown out,
For throwing them and being a tout,
I hate tigers, don't you?

Andrew Woods (10)
Milltown Primary School

PET CATS

Wee pet cats
Love to eat rats
Cats leap
Cats sleep
Cats lie
And they cry
They peep
And they creep
Cats are kind
In your mind
Cats flitter
In the litter
Cats are funny
They hate honey
Cats love rats
I love cats.

Sarah Hazlett (9)
Milltown Primary School

SHARKS

Some sharks have fins,
Others have flippers.
Some sharks have rays,
Sharks don't like kippers.
Hammerhead sharks, rays below,
Little sharks play all day.
Daddy sharks work so low,
Mummy sharks stay at home.
Auntie sharks come to stay,
Uncle sharks work alone.

Sarah McAdam (9)
Milltown Primary School

CATS

Cats are silly
Name them Billy
Cats for a pet
Noses are wet
Cats are cute
Unlike a newt
Cats can see
So can we
Cats are funny
They like a bunny
I love cats
They sleep on mats
Cats love birds
They don't like nerds
Some cats are greedy
And some are needy
Some can yap
But I can clap.

Aimee Crothers (10)
Milltown Primary School

HOW ANIMALS MOVE

Lions prowl, wolves howl.
Dogs pounce, rabbits bounce.
Kangaroos jump, tigers hump.
Sharks leap, larks sweep.
Cats creep but bats sleep.

Tigers roar, pigs snore.
Worms wriggle, slugs jiggle.
Cheetahs run, but I slum.

Matthew Dickson (7)
Milltown Primary School

SOUND OR MOVE!

Lions roar
Larks soar

Kittens creep
Kangaroos leap

Horses neigh
Hens lay

Frogs hop
Horses clop

Monkeys swing
Bees sting

Lions prowl
Wolves howl

Birds swoop
Cats poop

Elephants amble
Dogs scramble

Fish hide
Snakes slide

Bells ring -
But I sing.

Amanda Aulds (8)
Milltown Primary School

HOW ANIMALS TALK AND WALK

Lions roar
Larks soar
Kangaroos bounce
Cats pounce

Dogs roll
Horses stroll
Camels leap
But I sleep.

Adam Johnston (8)
Milltown Primary School

HOUSE CAT OR A WILD CAT?

In the morning
She pounces up
On the bed
Where she sleeps

In the afternoon
On the window seat
She looks at the sun
Waiting for tea to come

In the evening
Out the front
She sees a mouse
Playing with another mouse
Slowly creeping up
She pounces on them both

In the night
In the fields
Catching mice
Is where she is

Now will you tell me
Is my cat a house cat
Or is she a wild cat?

Jenny Wallace (10)
Milltown Primary School

MY RABBIT

My little rabbit Lucy
Sits in her hutch all day,
I think that must be boring
Because there isn't enough room to play.
It was not our fault she chewed a cable
Or chased our guinea pig around the room!

My little rabbit Lucy
Gets in a terrible huff,
She does not like apples
But eats up all the carrots.
I feed her a dishful every morning,
But usually she takes it and throws it away!
Her fur is lovely and soft
And her tail is pure black and white.
She also likes eating dock leaves
If you post them through the bars of her cage.

Louise Robinson (9)
Poyntzpass Primary School

BRAVERY IS . . .

Bravery is . . .
Walking over a rope bridge,
Walking around a graveyard at night,
Letting an elephant out,
Walking into a garage without standing on the cat at night,
Smashing a window,
Going into an aeroplane,
Getting told off,
Getting pricked by a thorn.

Matthew Patterson (7)
Poyntzpass Primary School

MY BEST FRIEND

My best friend is as sharp as a door nail,
But two days ago she fell and has sores, she was also pale.
Then when she talks she's as active as a bee,
She doesn't wear glasses that means she can see me.

My best friend is as fit as a fiddle,
But when she laughs she won't stop to giggle.
She sends me messages for me to seek,
When I find it I always take a peek.

My best friend loves to make me laugh
Then her brother runs like he's going daft.

My best friend is a best friend,
She's as smart as ever.
Do you know the name of my friend?

Rebekah Denny (9)
Poyntzpass Primary School

FIREWORKS

F   ire, the funny fireworks move busily in the sky.
I   nspect the fireworks carefully because you don't want
    to lose a hand.
R   ockets *bang* up in the air like you have never heard before.
E   xploring the Catherine wheels going around and around.
W   atch Roman candles light up in the night.
O   ooh! Look out of the window, see the fireworks going up in the sky.
R   oaring rockets *bang* in the sky.
K   itty go to bed, there are no more fireworks!
S   o soon, the party is all over!

Samantha Boyd (9)
Poyntzpass Primary School

I Am Glad She's My Best Friend

I have a friend,
Her name is Rebekah.
Rebekah is a church singer,
Not a church bell ringer.
She sings as fluently as an angel,
She has brown, long curly hair.
She has a freckly face
And when she puts on make-up
She looks a disgrace.

When she rings me every day,
Sometimes I say, 'Go away!'
When I am hungry she shares,
When I am hurt she cares.
She never leaves me out,
She's as strong as an ox,
So that is really cool,
When bullies come she'll shout, *'Boo!'*
And then they'll run away.
So watch out big bullies
Because Rebekah's here today.

She gets everything she wants,
She really is a clone of me,
We're sort of the same,
Definitely not in heights.
She gets loads of frights about spiders.
We have the same instruments; piano, trumpet, tin whistle, recorder,
We really are the same,
I am glad she is my best friend.
When Rebekah's there I can always depend on her.

Holly Lockhart (10)
Poyntzpass Primary School

THE BESTEST FRIEND EVER

Laura is my best friend,
She is as sweet as sugar,
She never ever tells me lies,
She is always really happy.

Laura's eyes are as brown as bark,
Her hair as shiny as glass,
We always see each other in school
And we're always on the phone.

Laura has the same things as me,
We go to each other's house,
We both like pets especially dogs,
We both had dogs for pets.

We always go places together,
Places, trips and parties,
We always like to see each other,
We don't live far apart.

Laura is as good as gold,
She always is my friend,
She always shares things with me,
She is really the best.

Laura has been my friend for years,
She has always been there for me,
She is always as friendly as a dolphin
And she is the best friend I've ever seen.

Amy Liggett (9)
Poyntzpass Primary School

FUN WITH MY PONY

Shadow is my pony.
Shadow is so sweet.
Shadow is as soft as a dove.

Shadow is so like me.
Shadow likes ice lollies,
Apples, carrots and Mars Bars, so do I.
Shadow's socks are as white as snow.

Shadow is as good as gold.
Shadow's star face mark
Is as white as snow.
Shadow and I are so alike.

We love to jump so high.
We like to jump as high as a bird.
We like to race my friend on her pony, Molly.

We do two laps around the field
But my friend always wins
On her pony, Molly.

Victoria White (10)
Poyntzpass Primary School

THE LITTLE HAMSTERS

I had a hamster that was fat and thin.
He was brown and white.
He had a fuzzy neck that was nicer than mice.
His name was Pippy.
I had another hamster and it was called Spikey.
This hamster was black and white.
The special thing she had was a little baby hamster.

Neil Thompson (8)
Poyntzpass Primary School

MY BEST FRIEND!

My best friend is Keith,
He is as sensitive as a bunny,
He is as cunning as honey
And sharing as my mummy.

Keith is as funny as money and silly as Billy,
He sometimes is as kind as Nanny,
Keith helps us when we get hurt,
He reminds me of a doctor.

He is as happy as a bulldozer,
But when he is sad he is as white as snow,
But cheer him up and he will be good for you.

Stephanie Henry (9)
Poyntzpass Primary School

MY BIRTHDAY

M y birthday is in April,
Y oung ones get so excited.

B ig ones usually get money,
I   t is lots of excitement,
R ipping presents,
T earing cards,
H aving fun and playing fair,
D oor is knocking,
A untie is here,
Y ou are the best niece there could ever be!

Claire Hamill (8)
Poyntzpass Primary School

THE BEST DAD

My dad
Is never mad.
He is as fit as a fiddle
And hates being in the middle.
He hates the doctors
And is interested in helicopters.

He likes biography
And Chelsea FC.
He is as intelligent as a whale
And sometimes puts up kale.
He cares about everything
And always likes to sing.

My dad earns a living
And likes riveting.
He is as kind as a dolphin
And doesn't like gin.
He likes steak,
But hates going to a wake.

He has ginger hair
And always likes to share.
He is as inventive as an inventor,
He would hate to be a janitor
And that is my dad,
The kindest man in the world.

Josh Ferris (11)
Poyntzpass Primary School

FOOTBALL

Football is lots of fun
When you play it in the sun.
Arsenal is my best team
And sometimes they are in my dream.

I play football against other schools
And we all have to obey the rules.
When we go away to play a match
I would like my friends to come and watch.

Robert Boyd (9)
Poyntzpass Primary School

MY SISTER

I have a friend,
She is my sister,
Her name is Louise,
She giggles,
She wiggles
And she is just full of life.
Sometimes she is as crafty as a fox
And when she's happy she acts like a cock,
She's an angel,
Then I'm in danger when I get on her nerves.

We share money,
That puts us in the mood for honey,
She winks her eye,
Then gives a little smile.
She helps me at home,
Then gives me a hit with her toe
And tells me to wise up,
And I say I give up.
I sing songs on my karaoke,
Then my sister comes along,
We sing songs together,
Then we have some fun,
I'm glad she's my sister.

Lindsey-Anne Henry (10)
Poyntzpass Primary School

JACK WILSON

My best friend is called Jack Wilson.
Jack goes to Mullavilly Primary School.
Jack works as fast as a bulldog.
His work is neat as a teacher.
Never is as bad as a bad boy.

Jack and I play together as brothers.
Jack is as fast at swimming as a speedboat.
His favourite work is art because he draws as an artist.
Jack helps me with work like a teacher.
He is kind and keeps an eye on me like a doctor.

His kindness to me is like a parent.
Jack lends stuff to me like an adult.
We both take walks as a family.
When I am sad he cheers me up like an uncle.
We spend time in school like policemen.

Jack comes on holiday as a tourist.
He lends money to me as a neighbour.
Jack shares sweets as a shopkeeper.
He sends presents as a guest.
I trust Jack as a father and a son.

Paul Hamill (11)
Poyntzpass Primary School

MY PET DOG

My pet dog ate a giant green frog
When I took it for a walk yesterday.
I took it to the vet and gave it a pet,
It chased a jet, that was a good pet.

Neil Anderson (9)
Poyntzpass Primary School

MY BEST FRIEND

My best friend is called Conor Copeland,
He is also my cousin,
He is very caring
And he is as friendly as a fireman.

When we are playing football
He always likes to score the goals,
But I think he should be in midfield
Because he is as tough as Tyson.

We like to play on the computer,
Sometimes we play on it for most of the day,
But when it comes to watching TV
He is as quiet as a mouse.

When we are talking to each other
We usually start to talk about WWE,
I think he should be a wrestler
Because like I said he is as tough as Tyson.

You can always trust him
Because he has never let me down
And I know he never will,
Because he is my best friend.

He lets me borrow his things
And I am never afraid to ask,
Because I know he will lend it to me
Because he is as kind as a cricket.

Steven Hendron (10)
Poyntzpass Primary School

MY BEST FRIEND

My best friend is Grace Wilson,
She's always there for me.
If I should fall
She would be there.
As fast as a leopard.

If she would come to my house
For a sleepover
We would put on music
As loud as a band,
Then start to jump on my bed.

I might tell her a secret
Or she might tell me one,
We would always promise
To keep the secret to ourselves
Then she would be quiet as a mouse.

She has green eyes,
She has brown hair
And she is quite small,
But none of this matters
She's still my best friend.

Naomi Clarke (10)
Poyntzpass Primary School

MY BEST FRIEND

My best friend is as good as gold,
Thankfully he is not as mad as a hatter.
My best friend taught me chess,
He'd never make a mess.

My best friend is as fast as a ferret,
I can't beat him in a race.
My best friend is as tough as an ox,
He loves to talk about pets.

He's as pleased as punch when he wins at chess.
He never picks a fight.
He can be as steady as a stone.
We go to scouts together.

My best friend is as cunning as a fox.
He's certainly not as round as a barrel.
My best friend, can't you guess?
It's Andrew Henry of course.

Kyle Robinson (10)
Poyntzpass Primary School

THE BESTEST FRIEND THERE COULD BE

My best friend is called Amy,
She is as sweet as honey,
She is as clean as money
And as nice as Mummy,
But very very funny.

Her hair is as brown as brown could be,
Her eyes are as brown as coffee,
Her lips are as pink as a daisy opening.

She is as honest as my brother,
As kind as my mother,
She is not that much bother.

She is sometimes cunning,
All that I can say,
That she is the *bestest* friend there could be,
She is the *bestest* friend for me,
On this very day.

Laura Megaw (9)
Poyntzpass Primary School

My Best Friend

My friend Tyrone makes me laugh nearly every day,
He runs like a rocket and jumps like a rabbit,
Well he likes tractors, maybe I like them too,
He's good as a best friend.

I talk to him every day, he always make me laugh in the class,
There's something about Tyrone that always makes me laugh,
He always makes faces in the line
But nobody sees him except Mr Doyle.

He always keeps people going,
I always sit beside Tyrone on a trip,
He likes Liverpool in the Premiership,
Well that's what friends are about.

Andrew Henry (11)
Poyntzpass Primary School

John Deere

J   is for John Deere,
O   is for Omagh town,
H   is for Harold Walker, he thinks they are the best,
N   is for narrow roads.

D   is for diesel, I need it a lot,
E   is for enormous, wow it is big,
E   is for exhaust, watch it is hot,
R   is for reverse, woah!
E   is for exhausted, good night.

Kyle Walker (8)
Poyntzpass Primary School

In School

I n our lovely warm school we play.
N ames our called out - Claire, Johanna, Rachel and Louise.

S tories are fun and poems are read.
C laire, Johanna, Rachel and Louise are my friends.
H olidays are given at school.
O h lovely, lovely, lovely school.
O n the
L ast day of school everybody is happy.

Cathy Wilson (9)
Poyntzpass Primary School

My Own Theme Park

My own theme park is really cool,
I love to dive in the swimming pool.
My rides are fab,
My shops are great,
So don't forget to bring your mate.
If you were here what would you do?
Would you go on the old log flume?
The biggest drops, lollipops
And lots of restaurants too.
But then I heard my sister cry,
I really thought, *oh why, oh why?*
I got out of bed and saw
Not my theme park standing there,
But my room full of toys.

It was all a theme park dream.

Liam Gray (10)
St Colman's Abbey Primary School, Newry

OH TO BE A FOOTBALLER

If I were a football player
I would play for Liverpool,
Oh, it would be so cool
Just to beat David Beckham
And Rivaldo to win
The Champions Cup,
How great that would be.

My sister, she would go crazy,
Scream like a banshee,
She hates Liverpool
And hates me.

I would play with Owen,
With Heskey it would be good,
For we would beat Man City,
Man United too, Newcastle and Everton
To go right to the top.

Jonathan McNamee (10)
St Colman's Abbey Primary School, Newry

MY DOG

I have a dog named Darkey,
He hasn't any sense,
When I'm setting off to school
He tries to jump the fence.

He growls and growls and barks a lot
Until I come back home,
But when he sees my face again
He knows he'll get a bone.

Kieron Markey (10)
St Colman's Abbey Primary School, Newry

FERRARI 550

My car is fast, red and roars like a lion,
When I sit behind the wheel
I am a rally driver with very steady hands,
My head is clear and my eyes are sharp
As the car twists and turns in the deep lumpy sands.

My foot pumps the floor and my hand grips the door,
The engine is soft just like a kitten
Purring and revving with a great deal of glee.

The exhausts are dark with the smell of smoke
And nobody ever thinks this car is a joke!

The name of my car is a Ferrari 550
And I'll say the name again with pride and glee.

Stephen Goodman (10)
St Colman's Abbey Primary School, Newry

MY PETS

Some of my pets stay in a cage,
Sometimes they fly about in a rage.

Some of my pets stay in a tank,
The look on their faces are always blank.

Some of my pets stay in a hutch,
They have a bad habit of eating too much.

Some of my pets stay in the yard,
Sometimes you see their pictures on a birthday card.

My last pet sometimes stays in the house,
She sometimes brings a visitor, a little grey mouse.

David Ruddy (9)
St Colman's Abbey Primary School, Newry

STADIUMS

Hot dogs,
Autographs,
Footballs,
Hats and scarves,
How I'd love to have these things.

Crowds,
Pitches,
Photos,
Flags,
I'd love to seem them all.

Highbury,
Old Trafford,
Anfield,
Elland Road,
I love the stadiums,
They're full of fun,
I wish I could go there every month.

David McCabe (9)
St Colman's Abbey Primary School, Newry

ONI

Oni is my favourite game,
It's hard to master fighting.
Konoko is a spy.
Before I play the game
I say, 'Good luck Konoko.'
I feel the game is hard for me,
But I play it again and again,
Then I find it easy.

David Shi (10)
St Colman's Abbey Primary School, Newry

HOLIDAY TREAT

Reading my book
While sitting in my seat,
Thinking of my holiday,
Oh what a treat.

Down on the beach
With my bucket and spade,
Or maybe I'll just
Stay by the pool instead.

Jump into the pool
Or jump into the sea,
Chinese or McDonald's
It's up to me.

Going to the zoo
And the water park too,
So little time,
So much to do.

When I awake
I look all around,
There's my homework book
Lying on the ground.

It was only a dream,
It wasn't a treat
But perhaps into the summer,
Now that would be neat.

Gavin O'Hare (9)
St Colman's Abbey Primary School, Newry

NIGHT ECHOES

I hear a noise in the night
But what could it be?
All night I hear it cry,
Searching for food that isn't there,
Crying and crying all night long.

I see a blink of something
But it's gone in a flash.
Perhaps it found some food, but where?
I will look in the morning,
Maybe find out what it is.

The next night all is silent
But still I'm scared
Of the noise in the night.

Conor Grimes (9)
St Colman's Abbey Primary School, Newry

SPRING

The chirps of the wild birds
Fill us with cheer,
Letting us know that summer is near.

The first flowers that peep
Are so lovely to see,
Giving much pleasure
To you and to me.

The days gradually get longer,
There's more time to play,
Leaving all my homework
To the end of the day.

Ryan Kearney (9)
St Colman's Abbey Primary School, Newry

OH TO HAVE A BOBSLEIGH TEAM

Oh to have a bobsleigh team,
How wonderful it would be
To skid down the slippery, icy hill
Like a ship on a stormy sea.

The sound of metal scraping ice,
'We're getting there in record time.'
I open my eyes and I can see
I'm flying past the winning line.

But sadly reality's suddenly here
When I hear my mummy's voice,
'Get up for school you sleepyhead.'
She gives me no choice.

Conor Fearon (9)
St Colman's Abbey Primary School, Newry

WHO?

He is . . .

As short as a dwarf,
As evil as an ork,
As terrible as a troll,
As eager as an elf.

As deadly as a dragon,
As gruesome as a goblin,
As ugly as an ogre
And greater than a god.

John Davis (10)
St Colman's Abbey Primary School, Newry

MY PUPPY

I have a little puppy
He is just two weeks old,
He is nice and fluffy
And very cuddly too!

His name is Timmy
And his father's name is Jimmy,
He is black and white
And he doesn't bite.

He lives in a kennel,
He has a bone
And a toy plane,
He sips his milk from a little bowl
And in the garden he likes to roll.

Christopher Hughes (9)
St Colman's Abbey Primary School, Newry

FOUR WHEELS AND A PLANK

Four wheels and a plank of wood outside the shop,
There it stood in the window, it stood proud.

The brand new skateboard its colours loud,
I had to have it to stand out from the crowd.

I counted my money
But it wasn't funny.

Not enough in my piggy bank,
I'll have to go back to my four wheels and a plank.

Ryan Campbell (10)
St Colman's Abbey Primary School, Newry

THE FOUR SEASONS

When springtime comes
And buds start to show,
The days get longer
And flowers start to grow.

Then summer arrives
And the sun shines down,
That's when we go to Bettystown.

When leaves start to fall
We know autumn is here,
With pumpkins in shops,
Hallowe'en is near.

As nights get dark
And the weather gets cold,
Ice, frost and snow,
I wish winter would go.

James Flynn (9)
St Colman's Abbey Primary School, Newry

SPIDER

Black and scary,
Big and hairy,
He fills us full of fear.
If he is there
You'd better beware.
He loves to give you a fright
So lock doors and windows
Or he might
Just give you a bite.

Paul Dillon (10)
St Colman's Abbey Primary School, Newry

OH TO BE A MILLIONAIRE

Oh to be a millionaire,
How fantastic it would be
To spend my millions wildly
On a crazy shopping spree.

I'd buy a jazzy, flashy watch
Or those new football boots,
I'd buy my mum a diamond ring
And my dad a Gucci suit.

I'd probably fly Concorde
Way across the sea,
I'd book up every single seat
For my friends and family.

Then I'd stretch out on the beach
Soaking up the sun,
Dream happily of my millions
Each and everyone.

Now my dreams are over
Reality has set in,
I'll crumple up my Lotto ticket
And throw it in the bin.

David Morgan (10)
St Colman's Abbey Primary School, Newry

MIRROR LAND

In Mirror Land I go to play,
Where I am happy, through the day.
In Mirror Land things are plain to see,
Bright and beautiful, the way life should be.

Skies are blue, mountains are green,
Trees are tall, no people are mean.
Happy faces, trusting smiles,
It's Mirror Land for miles and miles.

Ryan Archer (10)
St Colman's Abbey Primary School, Newry

UNDER THE BED

Under the bed is full of dust
And creepy crawlies too.
Watch out before they get you,
You don't know what they might do.
The dust could wrap you up and choke you,
The creepy crawlies could scratch your skin
And there are cobwebs and dirty socks too,
So never go under the bed.

Luke Wall (10)
St Colman's Abbey Primary School, Newry

WINTERTIME

Winter comes once a year,
Snowball fights I do not fear.
Icicles hang from the wall,
On the ice I fear to fall.
Little birds need lots of food,
We have to feed them, even in a bad mood.
Snowdrops in their flowerbeds,
Peeping up their little white heads.

Bobby Surgenor (9)
St John's Primary School, Hillsborough

MY DOG

My dog is called Shep,
He is my pet,
He hates cats,
He likes to play every day,
Even if it's not a nice day
He plays anyway.
He likes to eat bones, he moans,
I feed Shep every day
Even when I go away.
I play with balls, Shep hides all of them,
He goes to sleep,
When he wakes up
My daddy is mad,
He says that Shep is bad,
Now my story has to end.

Hannah Morrow (7)
St John's Primary School, Hillsborough

MY CAT

My cat is fun,
She likes to run,
She lies under the sun.

She had four kittens
But they got lost
And now she's having more.

The Tom cat comes round,
We don't know his name
But he's very tame.

Amy Robinson (7)
St John's Primary School, Hillsborough

SPRING

Spring, spring is here at last,
Winter days are really past.
The buds are shooting
And the owl is hooting,
The birds sing . . .
Hooray, hooray it is spring!
The cows they are so very glad
They rush out like mad.
Hedgehogs awake from their sleep
And round the door of their nests they peep.
Out of their nests they come
With an empty tum,
Hungry to find some food
But in a bit of a sleepy mood.
The birds are cheeping, *cheep, cheep, cheep,*
While they build their nests tidy and neat
And the lambs are going, *bleat, bleat, bleat.*
The baby foxes are playing while it's sunny,
When they finish I bet they'll try and catch a bunny!
The horses are so happy they go, *neigh, neigh*
While they're eating the last bits of hay.

Anna Martin (9)
St John's Primary School, Hillsborough

BATS

Bats, bats are scary and black,
With pointed ears and a furry back.
They hang upside down and wear a frown,
They have sharp teeth and great big wings,
Bats sleep in the day and come out at night,
To give us all a horrible fright.

David Martin (7)
St John's Primary School, Hillsborough

MY KITTEN

I have a kitten,
Sometimes I've been bitten.
I love her very much,
She scratches me with just one touch.
She loves the snow,
She runs when I shout go!
I pat her every day
But get no pay.
She likes chasing mice,
We give her chicken, but just one slice.
She eats it up with a crunch, crunch, crunch,
She is happy when she gets her lunch.

Steven McClune (9)
St John's Primary School, Hillsborough

WINTERTIME

Winter comes once a year,
Come on, let's cheer, cheer, cheer,
There's lots of snow all around,
Building snowmen on the ground.

Throwing snowballs at everyone,
Lots and lots and lots of fun,
Slipping and sliding on the hill
Gives us all a great big thrill.

Everyone has to wrap up warm,
Here comes a great big storm,
Go inside and close the door
And you will feel the cold no more.

Rachael Robinson (9)
St John's Primary School, Hillsborough

MY CAT

I have a cat, her name is Bab,
I think she is absolutely fab,
We play together all day long,
In my eyes she's never wrong.
We play together in the hall,
I throw to her a little ball.
She likes to run and jump about,
Oh I wish that she could shout.
We sit together by the fire,
I stroke her fur and she goes *purr*
She is the best cat in the world,
My little fluffy best friend Bab.

Jordan Quigg (8)
St John's Primary School, Hillsborough

I CAN

I can jump over the moon,
I can jump over a balloon.
I can jump so high,
I can touch the sky.

I can bounce like a kangaroo,
I can bounce like a didgery doo.
I can bounce so well,
It is really swell.

I can fly like a bird,
I can float like a cloud.
I can swim like a fish,
Swimming in a dish.

Andrew Oliver (9)
St John's Primary School, Hillsborough

PONIES

Ponies are running in the grass,
Watch them as they go past,
Jimmy Jump, Stevie Boy, Nut Hill Star,
Don't forget they have lots of power,
I like ponies, they're lots of fun,
Especially when they run in the sun,
Jimmy Jump is black,
He doesn't wear a cap,
Stevie Boy is brown,
He deserves a crown,
Nut Hill Star
Will go very far,
He would eat oats for an hour,
Off to Danescroft in the pouring rain,
Will Jimmy Jump win again?
Jumping quickly against the clock,
If he hits a pole, it will surely rock.

Rhianne Dillon (10)
St John's Primary School, Hillsborough

THE OLD OAK TREE

Is it big or is it small?
Is it old or is it tall?
The leaves so green, the tree so brown,
Is it in or out of town?

The sparkle it gives in the bright day,
'I wonder what it's like at night,' they say.

Joanna Guthrie (9)
St John's Primary School, Hillsborough

CARTOONS

Cartoons are funny just like little bunnies,
They jump around and make a big sound.
When they ping and they pong they always
Sing a song so they always say hello all day.
All the cartoons are like baboons they climb up
Trees and they always sneeze.
There are some funny and there are some chubby
There are some thin and some fat but there's always
A black cat.
There are some that can fly but the fly is a pie
I can't understand why the cartoons are in a band.
The cartoon girls are cute but they don't always look
The cartoon boys are little devils but they
Always go down one level.
The cartoon dads always mow but they always say hello
The cartoon mums always wash with
A mop that says, 'Flip, flop, flip, flop.'

Hannah Walker (9)
St John's Primary School, Hillsborough

QUADS

Quads come in all different sizes,
50, 80 and 125
Quads come in all different makes,
Banshee and blasters, they are great,
They have four wheels and two brakes,
They have loads of speed,
Race them
Fix them
And race them again.

Richard Cousins (10)
St John's Primary School, Hillsborough

MY PET BOOMER

My pet Boomer is a lovely pet,
But he likes to escape every
Chance he can get.
We play catch but we're
No match for this is a very
Clever rabbit.
Boomer is as black as soot
And very, very cute,
In fact he is the coolest dude
In the neighbourhood.

I love him to bits even though
He nips but then he's a rabbit
With attitude.

Bruce Moulds (10)
St John's Primary School, Hillsborough

TRACTORS

Tractors are big, red, yellow, green and blue,
They'll get you out of a big wide ditch!
Good for you!
My dad hates tractors because they are
Big and slow, they take up all the room
But they are so cool,
When I am bigger, I will have a farm,
With a big green tractor, pulling trailers
Through the mud, ploughing fields with a meal,
I love tractors and so should you!

Michael Allen (10)
St John's Primary School, Hillsborough

BOYS!

Boys are the worst
They would make you burst
There is one boy called Harry
I wonder if he will marry
He drives me up the wall
He is quite tall
There is a boy called Andrew
He jumps right at you
There is this other boy called Mark
I think he is afraid of the dark
Harry for one thinks he is a hunk
But he's more like a punk
Mark thinks he's cool
But he's a fool
And Andrew, there's not much to say
But he sits beside me every day!

Rachel Morrow (10)
St John's Primary School, Hillsborough

BIRDS

Birds are such lovely creatures
And with soft feathery features.
My favourite is the eagle
I think it's better than a beagle.
All the owls I like them very much
And they are very nice to touch.
The kingfisher is such a good dipper
I wonder if it would eat a kipper?
I like to draw pictures of birds
And I hope the birds will like these words.

Matthew McClune (10)
St John's Primary School, Hillsborough

LITTLE MO

I own a little dog, her name is Little Mo
And every time I go walking,
She comes behind on tow,
She likes to play hide and seek,
She sometimes nicks my slippers
And then begins to lick my feet!
In the mornings, before I go to school,
She comes into my room to wake me up,
I love this part of the day when Mo
Comes in to play.
At night I make her tea and she cuddles
Up on my settee, she's like a little rug
All warm and furry, brindle and white,
My Little Mo is a bit of alright.

Kerry Moulds (8)
St John's Primary School, Hillsborough

DOGS

My friend Karen has a dog called Candy,
She has a coat that is the colour sandy,
My dogs are called Spike and Molly,
The girl dog's second name is Holly
And she is a type of collie,
My granny and granda have a dog called Rico
He doesn't like to drink cappuccino
My other friend Kerry has a dog called Mo
Recently she had a photo and I think she
Wore a bow.

Caitlyn Kennedy (8)
St John's Primary School, Hillsborough

FOOTBALL

Football is the greatest kind of sport,
But before we start playing, there are
Things we have to sort,
Picking the teams is a difficult task,
'Am I playing?' the players all ask.
A healthy diet is what they need
To play football you need a good feed
And finally when you go out to the pitch,
If you get an injury, you might need a stitch,
After a game you might have a ball,
Or you might feel quite appal . . . led
In the dressing rooms there's always fun
Where you have champagne and a bun.

Nicholas Kennedy (10)
St John's Primary School, Hillsborough

CANDY . . . MY DOG!

Candy is my dog
And I love to take her for a jog.
Candy loves the snow
When I tell her to run, she . . . go . . . go . . . goes.
Candy loves her toys
And she likes boys!
Candy likes to have a pat
I wonder if she likes cats.
Candy loves her food
That is very, very, good.
Candy's very nice
She chases away all the mice.
Now I have to say goodbye
To teach her tricks . . . at least I'll try!

Mark Thompson (9)
St John's Primary School, Hillsborough

My Last Year At Primary School

It is my last year,
I am really sad,
So I will never forget my friends,
For I am leaving this year,
I think I will fear a tear.

My brothers and sisters,
Will still be there,
But they are all amalgamating to a new school,
The boys in my class I'll miss them very much,
Even though they are a pain.

Some of the boys in my class will be going to the same school as me,
But some will not be,
I will miss my primary school so very much.

So from me to all the school, goodbye,
Because I will miss you so very much.

Chelsea Walker (10)
St John's Primary School, Hillsborough

Winter

Winter is cold,
Birds fly away,
Except for the robin . . .
It will stay!
Hop, hop, hopping,
Happy as can be,
It has a red breast,
Can you see?

Karen Thompson (7)
St John's Primary School, Hillsborough

SCHOOL IN WINTER

School in winter, what a bad thing to happen,
Day one, too cold to go outside so we stayed inside
Doing work.
Day two, so bad outside, your fingers will fall off,
Day three, I'm going mental, three days inside,
Day four, no fresh air, in four days too much work,
Day five, help me! Too much work - me mad,
Day six, home at last, no more school!
What - that was the first week
No!

Lawrence Boyd (11)
St John's Primary School, Hillsborough

HULLABALOO

My dad is a great guy
If I were shopping it's he I would buy,
I think he is fantastic,
Although he may score low in gymnastics.

He's as funny as can be,
He tells jokes to my sister and me,
Though he sometimes drives me up the wall,
He's the one who picks me up,
When I fall.

My dad is handsome and he's tall,
He is the best dad of them all,
I really love him, oh so much,
He is so kind and he has such a gentle touch.

Eimear Boyle (9)
St Laurence O'Toole's Primary School, Newry

HULLABALOO

I have a dog
He is as fat as a hog
He is really lazy
And sometimes he goes crazy.
He eats my hat
Along with my mat
What do you think, just fancy that.

He chews our doors
And licks our floor
And my ma goes mad about the scores
On the door,
When I'm playing with him and having fun
I try to lift him but he weighs a ton.

Seanin Smith (10)
St Laurence O'Toole's Primary School, Newry

HULLABALOO

My cat is black and white,
It purrs at night
And often gives me a fright.

One night it went berserk,
It ran around the house,
Trying to catch a mouse.

Things got really worse,
When I tried to intervene,
The cat scratched me,
It was an awful scene.

Miceal White (10)
St Laurence O'Toole's Primary School, Newry

HULLABALOO

This morning in our house
Things went crazy because of a little mouse
This mouse appeared on the floor
Which caused a very serious uproar.

Dad ran for the brush
Mum took flight in a big rush
My sister screamed as loud as could be
My brother frantically spilled his tea.

I stood still afraid to move
Hoping things would soon improve
The little mouse vanished into the blue
After creating such a *hullabaloo!*

Helen Murphy (10)
St Laurence O'Toole's Primary School, Newry

HULLABALOO

We were on our way to Salou
But unfortunately I got the flu
Mummy did not know what to do
She sent me home and Daddy too.

I had such a boring time
But after a week I was fine
I couldn't wait until they got home
But then I answered the phone.

Mummy said our plane is delayed!
We won't be home for a few days!
'It's all one big hullabaloo
And I think Caoimhe has also got the flu!'

Lorcan Quinn (10)
St Laurence O'Toole's Primary School, Newry

HULLABALOO

Years and years and years ago
The world was fresh and green
Trees were tall and the sand was clean
The air was fresh
And made you smile
So people walked for miles
And miles.

But in this year 2003
The world is a sorry sight to see,
Many animals die because of this,
At the cost of our own bliss.

Smog and smoke pollute the air
While people now don't even care
The mountains of rubbish
Grow and grow and the Green party
Say I told you so.

Aoife Deighan (10)
St Laurence O'Toole's Primary School, Newry

HULLABALOO

It was a dark, stormy, winter's night,
As I lay sleeping in my bed
I woke up and got such a fright,
A ghost was looming above my head.

I screamed and ran towards the light
And hoped he would go
But what a horrible scary sight,
He was still swaying to and fro.

He flew behind me and shut the door tight,
He was really very mysterious
By now I was really furious.

The ghost he was about my height
So I thought I'd take him on,
I fought with him and put up a good fight
And suddenly he was gone.

Kelly McKeever (9)
St Laurence O'Toole's Primary School, Newry

HULLABALOO

Home from school
Homework time
Have to get it done,
Then it's into
TV land,
Time to have some fun!

First Art Attack,
Then Fingertips,
Next a teenage witch Sabrina!
With her talking cat
And her crazy aunts
I wish I could have been her!

My Parents,
They are aliens
It's very funny too -
But my favourite one
Just has to be
That dog called Scooby Doo!

Shannon Hughes (9)
St Laurence O'Toole's Primary School, Newry

THE SHADOW

The wind was blowing very strong.
Something seemed to be terribly wrong.
Eerie sounds could be heard all around
And the moon it hid behind the clouds.

As I was stealing into bed
And nodding off to sleep,
I felt something touch my head,
A shiver ran down to my feet.

I sat up and looked around,
Afraid to put my feet on the ground,
But I saw nothing there
So I tiptoed to the door
And crept down each stair.

A shadow appeared to cover me,
As it slithered across the wall,
But in the black, inky darkness,
I could see nothing at all.

I could feel two eyes upon me,
My confidence seemed to crack
And then, at once I felt
Five icy fingers on my back.

I screamed out loud and ran and ran
Until I thought my heart would stop.
I froze dead in my tracks,
Wondering what was there.

But as I told myself, it had all been a dream,
A throaty laughter filled the air.

Clare Rooney (11)
St Macartan's Primary School, Downpatrick

SNOW DAY

The whole town is covered,
In a blanket of snow,
Then the first sign of life,
Starts to show.

A robin looks around
And finally comes down
And then a mouse
To see what he can scrounge.

And all of a sudden,
Some children burst out,
Trailing behind them,
Parents shout.

'Come back here this instant
Or there'll be no supper tonight.'
But the children do not hear them,
They're in the middle of a snowball fight.

All dressed in hats and gloves,
Sleighing down hill,
Making men and snow,
They can't be stopped until . . .

Oh no it can't be!
It has started to rain!
All the snow has melted
But we hope it comes again.

Anna Grant (11)
St Macartan's Primary School, Downpatrick

SCREAM

Eerie noises in the hall,
Big black shadows on the wall,
Chains clattering on the ground,
But there's no one to be found.

Footsteps on the stairs,
Could there really be someone there?
I lie in bed and stare,
I stare and stare, could there be someone there?

A hand on the door handle,
I see the flickering of a candle,
Then again the moving of the handle
And then I see the flame of the candle.

I lie and stare at the flame,
I see someone standing near,
But I do not know their name,
I do not like this game.

I suddenly wake from my sleep
And quickly take a peek,
It has all been a dream,
So I did not need to scream!

Danny Fitzsimons (11)
St Macartan's Primary School, Downpatrick

ONE SCARY NIGHT

Sitting beside the fireside,
I heard a large crack,
When I looked about,
There was not a might in sight,
Then I heard a sinister groan,
It sounded like something,

Slithering down the stairs,
Could it be Dracula
Or just a figment of my
Imagination?
Guess what it was?
The wind howling outside my window.

Stephen Kearney (10)
St Macartan's Primary School, Downpatrick

THERE'S A MONSTER ON MY ROOF

There's a monster on my roof,
A scary one I'm sure,
Tonight I hear him loudly howl,
I know this is no spoof.

There's a tapping on my windowpane,
Whatever could it be?
I'll cover my head to get to sleep,
Maybe that will ease the strain.

Under the covers I stay hidden,
Fearful of his wrath,
Please make this creature disappear,
His presence is forbidden.

If only my parents were not out,
Then I would feel so brave,
I'd rush outside and face the beast
And scare him off, no doubt.

Just then I hear the front door creak
And footsteps in the hall,
Then I hear my mum's voice say,
'That storm has passed its peak!'

Conor Corrigan (11)
St Macartan's Primary School, Downpatrick

WINTER

As I walk to my class a winter blizzard blows
Freezing winter days have come
And skies begin to snow.

Little robins eat dropped crisps
From the frozen playground
While children wait snug inside
Watching them scrounge.

Children have snowball fights
And sleigh on mountains of snow
But soon the happiness will disappear
And sorrow will come
For winter is now ended.

Caelainn Carson (11)
St Macartan's Primary School, Downpatrick

MY ROOM

My place, my space,
My mess, my rules,
I decide who come and goes,
I'm allowed to throw my clothes,
I can lie in it without a worry,
My mum says tidy,
But I'm in no hurry,
As long as I can play my PlayStation 2,
There is nothing in it I have to do,
I can tidy once a year,
A path through my floor, I sometimes
Clear,
But it's mine!

Patrick McKenny (11)
St Macartan's Primary School, Downpatrick

THE MATCH

Running down the field,
I see the net in sight,
Desperately wishing for a goal,
I run with all my might.
I see the ball fling through the air,
I know where I should be,
I catch the ball running to the net,
But no! The whistle sounds from the referee,
He says I have run too long,
Without toe-tapping or bouncing the ball,
He gives it to the other side,
It's their chance to even the score, 1 all,
But they miss out, without a doubt,
I see the ball come near,
I clear the field, running with speed
And yes, a goal and a cheer.

Brendan O'Neill (10)
St Macartan's Primary School, Downpatrick

MY PET

I have a favourite pet,
It's slimy and it's wet,
It flips about,
Looking to get out,
Just like a little scout.

Blowing bubbles on the top,
Jumping about like a little tot,
Blow, blow, bubble, bubble,
Just looking for a little trouble.

Amanda Magin (11)
St Macartan's Primary School, Downpatrick

SCREAM

Knocking on the door,
Howling, rattling I pulled the bed clothes,
Over my head shivering, shaking nervously,
Awaiting to hear the door,
Creaking open.

Then I hear footsteps,
On the floorboards,
My heart starts to pound,
I cannot stick this anymore,
So I crawl over to my bedroom door.

I gently open it,
I tiptoe out and look about,
Something touches me I turn away,
It gets a better grip of me,
Then I give a mighty
Scream!

Patrick McMullan (10)
St Macartan's Primary School, Downpatrick

THE SEA

I tell you a tale tonight,
Which a seaman told me,
With eyes that gleamed in the light
And a voice as low as the sea.

You could almost hear the stars,
Twinkling up in the sky and the old
Wind woke and moaned in the trees,
While the same old waves went by.

Suddenly the waves hit the rocks
And the sky got dark and grey,
Then the waves came crashing over us
And we knew this was the end.

Ashleen Gallagher (10)
St Macartan's Primary School, Downpatrick

WHAT'S IN MY ROOM

As I lay in my bed in the
Middle of the night.
I hear a noise that gives
Me a fright.

Was that the roof cracking
Or the wind at the door
Or was it something creeping
Along the floor?

I pull the blanket further
Over my head.
I'm sure there is something
To dread.

Coming closer and closer to me
What on earth could it be?
If only I had the courage to
Look out from the blanket to see.

Then it stops and I take a
Deep breath,
As I get ready to pull the
Blanket off my head.

Ready, steady, here I go
Aaahhh!

Ciara Cochrane (11)
St Macartan's Primary School, Downpatrick

MY NEIGHBOUR

Her clothes are black,
Her skin is white,
But damp and wrinkled.

She creeps around her haunted
House looking for . . .
No one knows!

Some people say it's her
Husband
Some people say it's her lost
Soul.

But I believe the red *paint*
Along her walls
Might explain
Something,
Don't you?

Emma Knight (11)
St Macartan's Primary School, Downpatrick

FEAR

Sometimes we get scared and wet the bed,
Sometimes we get scared when it gets to our head,
Is it in the cupboard or under the bed?
We hear a bang and a thump,
What's that big lump on my bed?
It's just my stupid brother falling out of bed.

Gemma Mackin (10)
St Macartan's Primary School, Downpatrick

HP . . .

I was looking in the shed,
One winter's night,
When I saw a shadow,
It gave me an awful fright!

Rattling and banging,
Something creeping about,
Blood dripping from the door handle,
What an eerie sight!

Now a weird noise,
Just like a burp,
It was my dad,
With half a burger
And red sauce
Everywhere!

Michael Brannigan (10)
St Macartan's Primary School, Downpatrick

BASKETBALL

B   asketball is a brilliant game,
A   ccurate shooting, 'What a point!'
S   hooting hoops and scoring points,
K   eeping the ball away from other players,
E   xhausted after playing so long, bring on the subs!
T   hree pointer, what a shot!
B   ouncing the ball round other players,
A   record for the most points, Boston Celtics win!
L   eaping up into the air, he's pulled off a slam-dunk!
L   eaning high over the other player to stop him from shooting!

Conor Smyth (10)
St Macartan's Primary School, Downpatrick

NIGHT CAMP

Packing up my rucksack,
My tent and my lamp,
Off we go into the woods,
To set up camp.

The howling of the wind,
Whistling through the tree,
I go out to have a look
And find two big eyes looking at me.

At first I am very frightened,
I want to go back,
But then I realised it was my dog,
Burying my rucksack.

Eamon Byrne (11)
St Macartan's Primary School, Downpatrick

THE RAINFOREST

The snake comes down
And the cricket just frowned
Down to the ground,
The worm is found
In the rivers
The croc sniggers
At the floor
It is dull and a bore
The jaguar flies
The bird spies.

Paul McWilliams (10)
St Mary's School, Saintfield

THE ICICLE

I am an icicle
Hanging from a wall,
'Drip, drip, drip,'
Says little boy Tom.
The sun comes out
And now I plop, plop, plop,
To the puddle beneath.
I'm melting, melting
Away to nothing.
Now Tom has broken me
Off the wall.
He has put me
In his back pocket,
He sits on the radiator,
I am dead!

Christopher McCormick (11)
St Mary's School, Saintfield

RAINFOREST

R   ainforest rap the place to be
A   nimals are everywhere and lots to see,
I   nside we see some wild buzzy bees,
N   one of the trees are free, free, free,
F   ind a baby animal jumping in a tree,
O   ther things are watching you so watch out the
R   ainforest animals are listening to you,
E   arly we go to hunt and play,
S   o go to the cave and stop, you see a
T   iger then you run and bang goes the gun.

Paula McGreevy (10)
St Mary's School, Saintfield

VALENTINE

Valentine's day is about love
And if you forget, they will still love you.
A special love you don't forget
On this special day.

Have an easy day, on Valentine's day,
No extra work for you,
So stay in bed, have a cup of tea
And we will dust and clean,
Sit down and just relax.

We promise to be good kids,
Nice flowers and chocolates just for you.
Everyone must be kind on Valentine's day
So enjoy your special day.

Jenny Carvill (9)
St Mary's School, Saintfield

WINTER'S COLOURS

Winter has so many colours
Most of them are black,
My friends, they just kid around
(With their white and silver sacks.)
All of winter's colours,
Are a very lovely
Sight but
Nothing beats the colours of a
Really hot fire.
The colours of a fire, sparkling red
And orange,
The heat you just can't stand it,
It is the colour you need.

Michael Mooney (8)
St Mary's School, Saintfield

GRANDMA AND ME

Grandma's my best friend
(But I just call her Win)
She's not the type of grandma
Who sits with her needle and pin.

We'd sit on the armchair
Look out the window and stare
At the white horses in the tide
And my best friend by my side!

She'd help me with all sorts of things,
Like exams, (chocolates) and strings,
I'd help her with the dishes
And sort out all the dirty fishes.

I love my grandma.
For she's my best friend
And everyone knows that friend
Ends with end,
But me and grandma
Our love will never, ever, ever,
End!

Susannah Wilson (11)
St Mary's School, Saintfield

WINTER

Trees are icy
Children play snowballs
Snow drops from trees
Fields covered in ice
Roads are slippery
I stay inside.

Marc Shannon-McCormick (7)
St Mary's School, Saintfield

A SNOWFLAKE

There I am in the sky
With all the clouds
They hit together
And I fall
What will I do?
Will I fall or will I die?
Slowly I fall
Closer and closer
The ground I can see
It looks so very hard
I am almost there
I have reached the
Ground at last
On a tree branch I land
And wait until the
Children come to see me.

Rachael Dalton (10)
St Mary's School, Saintfield

CHRISTMAS

C   hristmas is the best time of the year,
H   erald angels singing all around us,
R   eady to get your Christmas dinner,
I   nviting people to come to your house,
S   anta Claus comes to your house,
T   oys,
M   erry Christmas you say to everyone
A   nd you get Christmas pudding,
S   anta is coming round to see if you're sleeping at night.

Elisha Marks (11)
St Mary's School, Saintfield

SNOWFLAKE

Fragile as I am
Delicate as can be
Falling from the sky
Children watch with glee
I look at them and wink
I fall onto the road
I am happy when they play
When they run around and say
'I hope he never goes away,
Because we want him to stay.'
Then morning comes
The sun arises
They come out to see
I've disappeared
Where can I be?

Molly Mooney (10)
St Mary's School, Saintfield

SNOWFLAKE

This is how the snowflakes melt away,
When the sun sends out beams to play.
This is how they cover the ground,
Cover it thickly without a sound.
This is how the snowflakes blow in a heap,
Looking like little sheep,
This is how the people shiver and shake,
On an icy morning when they awake,
This is how the snowflakes fall.

In a lovely big white ball.

Heather McAllister (9)
St Mary's School, Saintfield

WINTER TREES

Icicles are hanging and falling from trees,
The trees are sparkling from tree to tree,
Shining like crystals shivering trees,
The ground is frozen and slippery,
The snow is dripping and melting,
Oh deary me,
Now it's just snowflakes falling.

On me!

Caoimhe Cassidy (8)
St Mary's School, Saintfield

THE RAINFOREST

The rainforest is very hot,
The snakes slither and slide,
The monkeys swing on the trees,
They try to catch the bees,
The birds fly about, sometimes they shout,
The rain is very hot, the monkeys think it's a lot.
The rainforest.

Bronagh Mullan (10)
St Mary's School, Saintfield

WINTER

In the winter when days go cold
Skies are grey and gloomy
Icicles dripping down from the trees
Snowflakes falling down from the sky
To make the ground a cloud.

Playing in the winter sun
I love to play and have some fun
Thinking of the sparkling days to come
When long winter days are gone
And Jack Frost is never there at dawn.

Orla Phillips (7)
St Mary's School, Saintfield

LOVE AROUND THE WORLD

It's Valentine's Day,
Love is in the air
With the little angels
Running wild,
Their mission to find some
Love around the planet,
Where there's true love,
You have to believe in yourself
To find it.

Donal Mageaan (9)
St Mary's School, Saintfield

SPRING

Spring bright and careful,
Lambs are born,
They're white and have black hooves,
Fields full of foul,
Nights are long and dark,
Days are warm and bright,
Children are out playing,
They are wearing heavy clothes.

Kimberley Kent (9)
St Mary's School, Saintfield

WINTER

The days get colder day after day,
That means we can't go out to play.
Snow is falling down,
Whitening the roads, the fields and the town.
The wind is blowing over the trees,
Each branch and twig bends in the breeze.
This is how the snow blows,
In a heap looking just like a fleecy sheep.
This is how the snow melts away,
When the sun sends out his beams to play.
This is how people shiver and shake,
On a snowy morning when they first awake.
This is how snow covers the ground,
Cover it quick without a sound.
This is how the snow plays about,
Up in the cloudland they dance in and out.

Samantha McQuaid (9)
St Mary's School, Saintfield

SNOWY'S FUNFAIR

At the funfair,
There are lots of sounds,
Roller coasters going up and down,
Roundabouts going round and round,
Shooting ranges going *bang, bang,*
Waterslides going *swoosh, swoosh*,
Bumping cars racing madly,
I ride on the typhoon, the best ride of all,
Getting wet on the log roll,
Best day of my life.

Eoin McKenna (7)
St Mary's School, Saintfield

WINTER TREES

It's dull and grey outside,
Ice hangs over the trees
And leaves are falling,
Swirling, swirling in the wind,
It's everywhere,
Ha, it's icy,
The trees are frozen,
Dripping snow making all of us slip and fall.

Jamie Hackett (7)
St Mary's School, Saintfield

ANGER

Anger is the colour red,
It looks like someone dying,
Anger feels like thunder crashing against you,
It smells like a forest burning,
It tastes like your tongue's on fire,
Anger sounds like a drill going through a wall,
Time to kill!

Chris Walton (9)
Towerview Primary School

WINTER

W ild howls in the night,
I   cy hands, feet and legs,
N   asty rain lashing down on the ground
T   rees so bare,
E   ventually the snow stops,
R   obins forever looking for food.

Aimée Samantha Graham (8)
Towerview Primary School

HAPPINESS

Happiness is the colour yellow,
It looks like the shining sun,
Happiness feels like a sunny holiday,
It smells like a daffodil,
Happiness tastes like vanilla ice cream,
It sounds like two birds singing.

Carrie Pyper (8)
Towerview Primary School

LOVE

Love is the colour red,
With hearts over your head,
It feels like someone cuddling you,
Love smells like fresh flowers in the garden,
It tastes like ice cream on a summer's day.

The sound of birds chirping all around,
Love, love all around the world.

Rebekah Kirk (8)
Towerview Primary School

ANGER

Anger is the colour red,
It sounds like thunder overhead,
It smells like burning rubber,
It tastes like burnt chips,
It looks like a volcano exploding,
It feels like dirty socks.

Ryan Kime (9)
Towerview Primary School

LOVE

Love is the colour red
It looks like a big red
Heart in front of you.

Love feels warm and soft,
Love smells like hot chocolate,
Love tastes like candy.

Adam Wilson (8)
Towerview Primary School

ANGRY

Angry tastes like sour milk in your tea
It sounds like thunder and lightning,
Angry is red like the sun,
It looks like a monster scaring people
Angry feels like you are being burned
Alive.

Beth Kernaghan (8)
Towerview Primary School

LOVE

Love is the colour red,
It looks like hearts everywhere,
Love feels all silky,
It smells like aftershave,
Love tastes like chocolate,
It sounds like kissing.

Andrew McCready (9)
Towerview Primary School

HAPPINESS

Happiness is the colour blue,
Happiness looks like the sun in the sky,
Happiness feels like a yellow flower.

Happiness smells like a hot bath,
Happiness tastes like apple pie,
Happiness sounds like the wind blowing.

Andrew Darrah (9)
Towerview Primary School

MY FAVOURITE THING

My favourite thing is my train set,
Click, clack as it goes round the track,
It soars all over my bedroom,
Red, black and gold blurs around
My room, peaceful and all mine,
The best toy ever.

Evan Fleming (9)
Towerview Primary School

LOVE

Love is the colour red,
It looks like someone getting married on a sunny day,
It feels warm and soft,
Love smells like a chocolate teddy bear,
It tastes like ice cream melting in your tummy,
Love sounds like birds singing on a tree.

Cory Rogers (9)
Towerview Primary School

FAVOURITE THINGS

My teddy Tiger is the best thing in the world,
Because it is orange,
Black, pink and white,
Orange, black, pink and white are my
Favourite colours,
He is the size of me
And he guards my bed.
He cost £9.99.

Glenn Wylie (9)
Towerview Primary School

WINTER

W inter is cold with icicles and snow,
I   vy and holly hanging from slipping trees,
N ails getting frozen by rain,
T   iny footprints about in the crisp snow,
E   very evening we snuggle in our cosy beds,
R   obins come to bury their food.

Erin Moore (7)
Towerview Primary School

WINTER

W ind swirling on the snowy trees,
I   cy icicles from the roof,
N ose red as the light bulb,
T   winkling stars at night,
E   very day I went outside and I saw a blanket of snow,
R   ed robins in the sparkling trees, beautiful.

Julia Tolerton (8)
Towerview Primary School

ANGER

When I feel
Angry, I get so
Blazen red,
I am so hot,
That I throw
My teddies around
The room.
Why does it have to be me?
Because I am grounded,
It is really boring!
How can I do this?
I want to be able to
Play with my friends
But I can't.
I whack the wall,
So hard and it hurts!
I shout to my mum so
Loud that my voice hurts,
I can't take this any more.

Amy Roylance (10)
Towerview Primary School

LONELINESS

Being alone is not the best thing,
Your face turns blue, grey maybe even green.

You feel sorry and sad, you want to talk,
To your mum and dad but don't know what to say.

It feels like eating ketchup, with chips on a plate,
I don't really like loneliness, it's happiness that's great.

Conor McClenahan   (9)
Towerview Primary School

FEELING HAPPY

When I feel happy
There is a glow of glory
And a flash of light.
When I'm happy
I feel glad all over,
It's better than
Feeling sad,
When I'm happy
Birds sing and there
Is a blue sky,
That's what it's like
To be happy.

Benn Laird (8)
Towerview Primary School

ANGER

When I am angry,
I go red like a fire,
The TV shakes in my room,
As I stamp on my feet,
I throw things of pain,
If they hit you,
I will tell you so
Stop I try,
But force too strong,
Still banging the doors,
Still pain to come.

Rhys Lundy (8)
Towerview Primary School

LONELINESS

When I feel lonely, I decide to read a book,
It makes me use my imagination to imagine
I'm in a faraway country with the sun
Beaming down on my back.

When I'm feeling lonely, I like to play the computer,
It cheers me up completely!

When I'm feeling lonely,
I like to play with my sister.
She is really kind.

I have expressed my feelings to you now -
I could have done it all day!

Jennifer Gouck (9)
Towerview Primary School

MADNESS

It looks like fire burning in your eyes,
It feels like lava.

It smells like something is burning all
Around.

It tastes like hot chillies burning in
Your mouth.

It sounds like people laughing
Ha, ha, ha.

Gustav Olaf Avenstrup (8)
Towerview Primary School

ANGER!

When I get angry,
I turn as red
As a volcano erupting.

I scream and shout,
Hit and kick my mum
She shouts at me, I yell back!

I get as mad as ever,
I start to throw things around.

I jump up and down on the floor,
My mum says stop it.

Now I am furious,
I can't stand it any longer!

Lisa Alexander (9)
Towerview Primary School

LONELINESS

When I am lonely I go
As blue as the sky,
I listen to music that I
Don't even like,
I listen to Elton John,
Sometimes I
Wreck my room.
I sit in the
Corner of my room,
Reading a book.

Alec Dobson
Towerview Primary School

THE WIND

The wind is roaring,
Crashing, bashing and howling,
I'm scared, I'm frightened, my door outside
Has even blown off and blown down town,
My dog is probably scared outside
All on his own, I wish I was out there with him,
The wind is roaring,
Crashing, bashing and howling.

Rebecca Irvine (8)
Towerview Primary School

THE LASHING WILD WIND

The wind outside was wild,
It was whistling and lashing on
My window. I wanted it to stop,
But it went on and on so,
I gave up, it would not stop,
But it did, when I went to sleep.

Luke Seawright (8)
Towerview Primary School

THE WILD CRASHING WIND

The whirling and spinning of the roaring bad wind,
Trees are blowing everywhere, left, right, up and down,
Crashing and smashing, blowing down the chimney,
Rattling against the flap blowing the ashes everywhere.

Ryan McMaster (7)
Towerview Primary School

THE WILD WIND

The spinning, whirling, flashing,
Roaring, crashing on the roof,
I was nice and cosy in my bed,
I was scared, all the pots outside
Were crashing down and smashing
On the ground, it was crashing on my window.

Rebecca Wright (8)
Towerview Primary School

WINTER

W indy skies every day we want to get out to play,
I cy trees with no leaves,
N ails are so cold with frost, frost, frost,
T rees are cold with tingling icicles hanging,
E veryone playing in snowball fights,
R ed robins looking for food but no worms in sight!

Amanda Hutchinson (8)
Towerview Primary School

SNOWY WEATHER

S now is icy and soft,
N ippy, cold, freezing snow,
O ld, crunchy, frosty snow,
W hite, bright, slippery snow,
Y ellow, snowy wellies.

Paige Morrow (7)
Towerview Primary School

WHIRLING WIND

The glittering, gluttering wind
Is blowing down the pots,
My shed door blew down and
I heard a big noise . . . *bang!*
When I was snuggled up in bed,
I was shivering and scared from head to toe,
The glittering, gluttering wind
Is blowing down the pots.

Portia Preston (7)
Towerview Primary School

SNOWY WEATHER

W indy wet weather feels very cold,
I   cicles dangling from my roof,
N   ippy Jack Frost is lurking about,
T   hunder crashes in the night,
E   venings are slippy and frosty too,
R   ain is scattering all over you.

Aaron McCausland (8)
Towerview Primary School

WINTER

W et wintry weather,
I   cy icicles on the roof,
N   orth wind in the air,
T   hunder roaring in the sky,
E   legant snowflakes in the air,
R   ainbow in the sky.

Rebecca McCormick (7)
Towerview Primary School

WINDY WEATHER

Birds fly south,
Hedgehogs curl in leaves,
Lightning strikes our house,
Snow covers the ground,
Icicles hanging from the roof,
Scattering elegant snowflakes,
Nights become short and cold.

Jamie Freeman (8)
Towerview Primary School

SNOWY WEATHER

Bright, sparkly, cold snow,
Wet, icy, smooth snow,
Squelchy, white sugary snow,
Freezing, damp, chilly weather,
Soft, freezing, crunchy snow,
Everything white and beautiful,
White trees blowing in the wind.

Sarah Gamble (8)
Towerview Primary School

ANCIENT EGYPT SNAKES

Slithering slimy scary monsters
Creep in the night,
You might see a glint,
Of its glowing red eyes,
The Egyptian people scatter,
The giant will make you feel frightened
Of its pointy black fangs.

Craig Andrews (8)
Towerview Primary School

SNOWY WEATHER

My cheeks are very cold,
I play in the snow,
All the ponds are frozen,
The ice is very slippy,
Snow is falling from the clouds,
Wrap up very warm,
My fingers are numb,
Ice is slippery and slidy,
Snow is very crunchy.

Louise Wylie (7)
Towerview Primary School

THE WEATHER

The sugary snow is falling,
The bright lightning is striking,
Freezing birds are flapping away,
The bright light of trees burning,
Fire is dying,
Squirrels hibernating,
Rabbits sleeping in peace.

Sara McDowell (8)
Towerview Primary School

SNOW

Squelchy snow,
Nippy, cold snow,
Sharp, crunchy ice,
White frozen snow,
Yellow wellies in the snow.

Shauna Armstrong (7)
Towerview Primary School

SNOWY DAY

Slushy, crunchy, icy snow,
Jack Frost is hanging
Around on this snowy day,
The children are out
Playing in the snow,
Their boots are squelching
In the snow,
It's windy and cold,
The children are wearing
Their hats, scarves and gloves.

Craig Norwood (7)
Towerview Primary School

MUD MASTER

A turnip muncher
A grass cruncher

A turned-up nose
A curly tail

A mud master
A clean disaster

A noisy grunt
A little runt

A catalogue
To make me . . .

A pig.

Cathy Berry (11)
Windsor Hill School

MY BEAUTIFUL DAYDREAM

My mum thinks I'm tidying my room
But no, I'm in a concert singing with Britney Spears
Or I'm taking a free-kick to win
The World Cup for England . . .
I'm in World War III or
I'm racing Michael Schumacher in a Ferrari . . .
I'm chasing Goldfinger.

My mum thinks I'm doing my homework
But I'm swimming with sharks . . .
I'm flying with the Royal Airforce or
I'm on a mission with Lara Croft . . .
I'm in a fight with a grizzly bear . . .
A spaceship is taking me to Mars . . .
I'm marrying Christina Aguilera . . .
I've broken Diego Forlan's legs.
'Stephen!'
Oh no, my daydream's over.

Stephen Murdock (11)
Windsor Hill School

SCHOOL

School is the place for me,
Where I do work and PE.
Mrs Craig is my teacher,
When in class she is the preacher.
I go outside to have a short play,
Some of my friends are Brian,
David, Kelley and Fay.

Stephanie Lilburn (8)
Windsor Hill School

DAYDREAMS

My brother thinks I'm playing,
But I'm racing in an F1 car
Or wrestling with the Rock.
I'm catching dinosaurs,
Or defeating pirates at sea.
I'm swimming with sharks,
Or making peace with aliens.

My brother thinks I'm listening,
But I'm teaching a monkey to write,
Or racing an octopus who can swim 100mph.
I'm playing football on the back of a plane,
Or flying a UFO.
I'm exploring the planet Mars,
Or I'm having a lightsabre fight with Darth Maul.
'David!' my brother said.
The daydream is over.

David Kernaghan (11)
Windsor Hill School

FEELINGS

I was looking out the window
And I saw an alien.
It said, 'Come with me.'
I stared at it.
It went into the garden.
We were playing a game, resist the pain.
That's what I see, a huge skull eating away at me.
It's only a dream or was it?

Colin Berry (11)
Windsor Hill School

A STRANGE BIRD

I saw a Phinox
Up a tree,
It looked at me
And giggled, hee, hee.

I stared at it
For quite some time,
It spat out lime
Which turned into slime.

My mum was cross
So she phoned her boss.
'I'm not going to work,' she said,
'My son's so sick he's away to bed.'

I soon got better
But without a letter.
I went to the woods and cut down the tree
And this time I was the one who giggled,
Hee, hee.

Alex Irwin (11)
Windsor Hill School

THE WEIRD BAT

I found a bat in the cupboard,
Think it must have come from a cave,
Because it's damp and black,
The darkness still in its eyes.

I gave it bits and bobs,
Tried seeds and bread,
But it looked at me trying to say,
'You don't know what food I need.'

It made a nest upon the bread
Even bigger than a rat's.
It does not belong there
And is very noisy.

If you want to see it
Come on round and peep,
But if you don't,
It will come to you!

Cheryl Park (10)
Windsor Hill School

DAYDREAMS

My mummy thinks I'm listening,
But no!
I'm making a song with Eminem,
I'm swimming with some dolphins
Or feeding panda bears.
I'm juggling with fire
Or an acrobat in a circus,
I'm racing on a highway.

My mummy thinks I'm working,
But no!
I'm lying on a beach in Spain,
I'm teaching a monkey to have manners
Or flying with tropical birds.
I'm feeding kangaroos,
I'm petting a small kitten
Or grooming a big dog.
My mum wakes me up,
My daydream is over.

Leanne Milne (11)
Windsor Hill School

JUNGLE JOKER

A mischief-maker
A banana taker

A tree swinger
A bad singer

An insect muncher
A banana eater

A jungle joker
An animal soaker

A catalogue
to make me . . .

A chimp.

George Moorehead (10)
Windsor Hill School

JENNIFER BATES

Jennifer Bates
Never shuts gates.
She's told every day
When she goes out to play,
To shut the gate and don't be late.
By the age of ten
She was told again and again,
But still she forgot
And forgot a lot,
To shut the gate and not be late.

Hannah Tate (11)
Windsor Hill School

THE LITTLE DRAGON

I found a tiny dragon hiding in my room,
It's small and green and friendly,
A little baby I assume.

It plays all day and stays awake all night,
A friendly little chap,
That won't give you a fright.

So please Mum, let me keep it,
I love it to bits,
If you say no,
It will give me fits.

I know only one thing when we go to sleep,
That when morning arrives,
Best friends we will keep.

Christopher Fullerton (10)
Windsor Hill School

DEADLY DEVIL

A rapid runner
A human stunner

A cave monster
A man-eater

A tree stomper
An animal muncher

A catalogue
To make me . . .

A dinosaur.

Dean O'Connor (11)
Windsor Hill School

MY DAYDREAMS

Miss Beck thinks I'm reading
But no, I'm shopping with Victoria Beckham
Or going to the cinema with James Bond.
I am in a sports car,
Or swimming with sharks.
I am teaching an elephant to play the piano
And Scooby-Doo to be a normal dog.
I go to school late, with
Elvis in my pocket,
Who I saw in the shopping centre.

Miss Beck thinks I'm listening,
But no, I'm in the middle of a
Record deal with Pete Waterman,
Or bungee jumping from the Empire State Building,
Or walking through a desert with a clown.
I am playing the main character in a horror movies,
I am in a speed boat with four dolphins behind me.
I am jumping off the back of a boat,
I think of doing a James Bond movie
Or singing with Pink or Busted.
I'm the new Batgirl, so Batman had better watch out.
I'm having lunch with Buffy the Vampire Slayer
Or I'm going to score the best hockey goal
That you have ever seen.
'What is the answer, Judith?'
Oh no, I've been caught.

Judith McCombe (10)
Windsor Hill School

FEELINGS

Happiness.
Happiness is yellow,
It smells like strawberries,
Happiness tastes like snow,
It sounds like a river,
It feels like water flowing.
Happiness lives inside you.

Anger.
Anger is dark red,
It smells like stinky feet,
Anger tastes like sour milk,
It sounds like a thunderstorm.
It feels like sick.
It lives everywhere.

Sadness.
Sadness is blue.
It smells like mouldy cheese.
Sadness tastes like rubbish,
It sounds like hammering,
It feels like ice,
It lives all around you.

Ashley Allen (10)
Windsor Hill School

WINTER

Winter is a time of fun,
A special time for everyone.
A time of love and joy,
When each child receives
A new toy.

Nicky Irwin (8)
Windsor Hill School

MUSICAL CATHY

There was a girl called Cathy,
Who always was so laughy.
A flute she plays
Or so she says,
That musical girl called Cathy.

Andrew Dalzell (10)
Windsor Hill School

THE BLUE TIT

I saw a little blue tit sitting on a tree,
I went outside to see if it liked me.
I gave it some food, but it flew away,
Then I noticed it came back the very next day!

Pamela McWilliams (10)
Windsor Hill School

THE MOON

The moon is white
All big and bright,
Floating in
The golden light.

Sean McParland (10)
Windsor Hill School

A Water World

A cliff smasher
A rock basher

A salt shaker
A wave maker

A water carrier
A world's barrier

A river's drain
A watery rain

A catalogue
To make me . . .

An ocean.

Ryan Lennon (11)
Windsor Hill School

Stealthy Slither

A champion fighter
A brilliant biter

A moving rainbow
A dangerous show

A rattling killer
A menacing thriller

A catalogue
To make me . . .

A snake.

Christopher McClelland (11)
Windsor Hill School

JUMPING KING

A hopping hurricane
A king kicker

A jumping athlete
A land snatcher

A plant muncher
An insect cruncher

A pouch protector
A Joey inspector

A catalogue
To make me . . .

A kangaroo.

Reuben Quinn (11)
Windsor Hill School

MY PET

My pet is a dog,
Her name is Millie,
You will always find her in a bog.

Millie is white,
White as snow
With blue eyes and a black nose.

Sometimes she's smart,
Sometimes she's silly,
That's my dog Millie.

Siobhain Butler (10)
Windsor Hill School

FEELINGS

Happiness.
Happiness is yellow,
It smells like strawberries,
It tastes like vanilla ice cream,
It sounds like the wind in the summer,
It feels like you're walking on air,
It lives inside a massive flower.

Anger.
Anger is red,
It smells like a rotten apple,
Anger tastes like red-hot chillies,
It sounds like a rusty chain,
It feels like a hot bath,
It lives inside a burning fire.

Amy Bell (10)
Windsor Hill School

WINTER

Winter is silent,
Winter is white,
Winter is cold
And might give you frostbite.

Winter is snowy,
Winter is fun,
Winter is slippy
So don't try to run.

Emerald Clyde-Stewart (8)
Windsor Hill School

FEELINGS

Danger is red.
It smells like burnt potatoes,
It tastes like wet chips,
It sounds like a storm,
It feels like a piece of chalk scraped on a board,
It lives inside a volcano.

Happiness.
Happiness is yellow,
It smells like flowers,
It tastes like milk,
It sounds like people laughing,
It feels like a summer's day,
It lives in Heaven.

Neil McMinn (10)
Windsor Hill School

THE DISCO BALL

The moon is a disco ball
Floating through the dancing air.

It is a silver 7-Up top
In the ocean.

It is a white ball
Thrown up in the summer sky.

It is a purple footprint
On a light piece of paper.

It is a broken clock face
Dropped down from the cabinet.

David Henry (9)
Windsor Hill School

FEELINGS

Happiness.
Happiness is gold,
It smells like tropical fruits,
It tastes like chocolate ice cream,
It sounds like birds singing,
It feels like a gust of fresh wind,
It lives in the middle of the sun.

Sadness.
Sadness is blue,
It smells like wilting flowers,
It tastes like icy-cold rain,
It sounds like the howling of wolves,
It lives in the deepest ocean.

Kirsty Auterson (10)
Windsor Hill School

FEELINGS

Happiness is golden,
It smells like a sweet apple,
It tastes like mint ice cream,
It sounds like birds singing in the spring,
It feels like a summer breeze,
It lives in the sun and sky.

Sadness is black,
It smells like a rotten apple,
It tastes like Brussels sprouts,
It sounds like a bang,
It feels creepy,
It lives in a gloomy cave.

Mark Jones (10)
Windsor Hill School

FEELINGS

Anger is red.
It smells like burning turf,
Anger tastes like rusty chains,
It sounds like an angry bull,
It feels like a boiling kettle.
Anger lives in a volcano.

Hope is yellow.
It smells like flowers,
It tastes like strawberry ice cream,
It sounds like bells pealing,
It feels like velvet,
It lives in your heart.

Andrew Baird (9)
Windsor Hill School

SHUT THAT GATE!

Jennifer Bates never shut gates,
At house number one,
The dog bit her bum.
That surely taught her.

Jennifer Bates never shut gates.
At house number two,
The cat had the 'flu.
The cat bit her leg,
She caught the plague
And all the gates were closed . . .
Forever!

Noelle Holmes (11)
Windsor Hill School

FEELINGS

Happiness is yellow.
It smells like real gold,
It tastes like ice cream,
It sounds like my heart beating,
It feels like gladness,
It lives in my heart.

Sadness is green,
It smells like burning fire,
It tastes like carrots,
It sounds like a thump on the door,
It feels like you've been trapped by a snake,
It lives in a volcano.

James Winton (10)
Windsor Hill School

SHUT THOSE GATES!

Jennifer Bates
Never shuts gates!
She went down a lane
And met her friend Jane.
They got into trouble
With Miss Hubble
Who told their mums
What they had done!
And then their mums yelled,
'Jennifer Bates and
Jane Wates
Start shutting gates!'

Naomi Meehan (11)
Windsor Hill School

FEELINGS

Happiness.
Happiness is red and orange,
It smells like strawberries,
It tastes like chocolate,
It sounds like the chirping of birds,
It feels like soft cloth
And it lives in your heart.

Anger.
Anger is dark scarlet,
It smells like burnt chips,
It tastes like cabbage,
It sounds like an erupting volcano,
It feels like you want to tear out your hair
And it lives inside you.

Matthew Kernaghan (10)
Windsor Hill School

FIONA MCLOOPING

Fiona McLooping
Is fond of snooping.
She sneaks round the doors
And crawls on the floors
Trying to find out
What everything's about.
To find out information,
She'll need concentration
And what she's looking for
Is her bedroom door
To sneak up on her cat
And grab her precious hat.

Christine Armstrong (11)
Windsor Hill School

FEELINGS

Happiness.
Happiness is yellow,
It smells like red roses.
Happiness tastes like strawberry ice cream,
It sounds like the birds singing,
It feels like you're flying,
It lives inside your heart.

Delight.
Delight is orange,
It smells like pink blossom,
It tastes like vanilla ice cream,
It sounds like robins chirping,
It feels like you're in the land of snow,
It lives in an apple tree.

Saloni Kapil (9)
Windsor Hill School

WINTER

Winter! The greatest season,
It is very pleasing.

Winter! I like to throw snowballs
At my friend, but he always falls.

Winter! There's lots of ice.
Winter! Which always makes me eat warm rice.

Winter! Wrap up against the cold breeze,
If you really don't want to freeze.

Oisin Jayat (9)
Windsor Hill School

FEELINGS

Anger is red,
It smells like dirty water.
Anger tastes like sour milk,
It sounds like an erupting volcano,
It feels like your head is about to explode,
It lives in a volcano with boiling lava.

Happiness is yellow and orange,
It smells like strawberry ice cream.
Happiness tastes like chocolate ice cream,
It sounds like water flowing by,
It feels like you're going to give someone a big hug,
It lives in the cloudy blue sky.

Holly McClorey (10)
Windsor Hill School

FEELINGS

Death is black,
It smiles like a dirty dog.
Death tastes like dirty sewers,
It sounds like a wolf howling at the top of a hill,
It feels like someone crushing their heart,
It lives in your soul.

Anger is red,
It smells like burnt potatoes.
Anger tastes like wet chips,
It sounds like a lorry on red diesel,
It feels like a mad dog eating,
It lives inside you.

Graeme Moffett (11)
Windsor Hill School

THE DAY AT THE BEACH

We went away in the car,
It was very far,
We were heading for the beach,
It took one hour to reach.

We looked up in the sky,
It was very high,
We saw the big, hot sun,
I knew we were going to have fun.

When we went down to the sand,
Lots of people were trying to get tanned.
I played with the seaweed
While Mum started to read.

I found a lovely stone,
Before we went home.
I went for a last run,
That was the end of the fun.

Johnny Kernaghan (9)
Windsor Hill School

SUMMER

Summer is sometimes hot
And I like it a lot.
Children are playing
And they all keep saying,
'Summer is the best,
It beats all the rest. Let's have some fun,
While we can enjoy the hot sun!'

Kelley-Louise Hunter (8)
Windsor Hill School

WAR

Why is there war?
I don't see the point of it.
Towns and cities are destroyed,
I don't like it a bit.
People get killed, like my pal, Loyd.
They are over silly things,
Like money,
Politics,
Could even be baked beans.
World War I, World War II
And loads more, before you know it,
There'll be World War III and IV.
So keep world peace on Earth,
We need to learn this from birth.

Alex Hanna (9)
Windsor Hill School

THE MOON

I sit by my window
I look up to the sky,
The stars shining bright,
Oh what a night.
A cloud moves by,
Is that the moon shining down on me?
It's huge! It's bright! My face all alight.
How I wish I was a star,
So I could be near the moon.

Robert Little (10)
Windsor Hill School

THE SUN

The sun is so bright
That gives us lots of light.
We play and have fun
In that bright, shining sun.

We can go to the pool,
That keeps us cool.
The sun will shine
Till about nine.

Stacey Moffett (9)
Windsor Hill School